Tech Prep Career Programs

In loving memory of Pauline Fagan

Tech Prep Career Programs

A Practical Guide to Preparing Students for High-Tech, High-Skill, High-Wage Opportunities

Revised Edition

Carol Fagan
Dan Lumley

CORWIN PRESS, INC.
A Sage Publications Company
Thousand Oaks, California

An earlier version of this book, titled "Planning for Tech Prep: A Guidebook for School Leaders" by Carol Fagan and Dan Lumley, was published by Scholastic Inc.

For information address:

Corwin Press
A Sage Publications Company
2455 Teller Road
Thousand Oaks, California 91320
E-mail: order@corwin.sagepub.com

SAGE Publications Ltd.
6 Bonhill Street
London EC2A 4PU
United Kingdom

SAGE Publications India Pvt. Ltd.
M-32 Market
Greater Kailash I
New Delhi 110 048 India

Printed in the United States of America

Library of Congress Cataloging-in-Publication Data

Fagan, Carol.
    Tech prep career programs: a practical guide to preparing students
for high-tech, high-skill, high-wage opportunities / authors,
Carol Fagan, Dan Lumley.—Rev. ed.
        p.   cm.
    Includes bibliographical references.
    ISBN 0-8039-6510-9 (acid-free paper).—ISBN 0-8039-6511-7 (pbk.:
acid-free paper)
        1. Vocational education—United States—Planning.   2. Technical
education—United States—Planning.   I. Lumley, Dan.   II. Title.
LC1045.F34   1996
374.246'0973—dc20   96-25388

This book is printed on acid-free paper.

97 98 99 00 01 02   10 9 8 7 6 5 4 3 2 1

Editorial Assistant:	Nicole Fountain
Production Editor:	Sherrise M. Purdum
Production Assistant:	Denise Santoyo
Typesetter & Designer:	Andrea D. Swanson
Cover Designer:	Marcia R. Finlayson

Contents

Acknowledgments

The authors would like to thank the Tech Prep Coordinators across the country who shared their knowledge and experience with us. We would also like to thank the Tech Prep Consortium of Johnson/Douglas Counties and Johnson County Community College in Overland Park, Kansas, for allowing us to use their materials within this manual.

On a more personal note, Carol Fagan would like to thank J. Riffel for advice and counsel, and G. Ross for support and patience. Saving the best for last, I thank my parents, who helped me understand that I can do anything.

About the Authors

Carol Fagan is Director for the Area Vocational School at Johnson County Community College in Overland Park, Kansas. She has 18 years of experience in postsecondary and secondary education as well as service with the Kansas State Board of Education. Carol has been involved in curriculum development at the local, state, and national levels. She holds a B.S. degree in Journalism and an M.A. in Speech-Communication.

Dan Lumley is Assistant Superintendent for the Spring Hill Public Schools in Spring Hill, Kansas. He holds a B.S.E. in Social Studies and an M.A. in Educational Administration. He also holds an Ed.D. in Administration and Foundations. A former teacher and curriculum director, he has authored and coauthored several books on technology leadership. A regular presenter at national conferences, he is currently focusing on school-to-work issues.

Introduction: Preparing Students for Careers

Educators have a responsibility to prepare students for the challenges of tomorrow. Those who work in or with secondary or postsecondary education have a unique mandate and a call to action: to prepare students for the high-tech, high-skill, high-wage careers that will allow them to successfully compete in our changing economy. It will take superintendents, counselors, curriculum co-ordinators, principals, teachers, deans, directors, and many others working together to achieve these goals.

We have been impressed with the changes that have occurred in the Johnson/Douglas Counties Tech Prep Associate Degree consortium schools since the beginning of our Tech Prep work. We have seen students and teachers come alive. More high school students are taking more math and science than ever before. This has increased the competency levels in these areas dramatically. One school reports students coming in before school starts (by choice) to work in the science/technology lab. Teachers, who were once isolated in their own classroom, are now team teaching, working on curriculum with their colleagues, and seeking new approaches to teaching. Students can now receive college credit for the technical classes they take during high school. If you want these kinds of changes to occur in your school, we highly recommend Tech Prep as a way to implement change.

Technical Preparation (Tech Prep) links high schools with community colleges and businesses to present a sequence of courses for students. This sequence provides skills for the growing occupations and careers of tomorrow. A Tech Prep program will provide a map for you as you change the way business is done in your school. The initiative requires planning, organization, and much endurance.

This book is written to help educators with little or no experience in Tech Prep. It presents a step-by-step process on how to plan, develop, and implement the program. It shows how schools can work collaboratively with businesses to organize programs that give students the core, technical, and specialty skills and proficiencies they need.

The first five chapters focus on learning about Tech Prep and getting started. Chapter 1 helps you understand the workplace which students will enter when they leave school. Knowing the challenges students will face allows educators to prepare them appropriately. Chapter 2 helps you focus your efforts on what is most important for your students. This chapter reviews how students benefit, how you can make Tech Prep work, and what you need to do to keep the program on track. Chapter 3 provides guidance on how you can organize your own consortium and begin to put the process in motion. Chapter 4 helps you define your own Tech Prep program and set some boundaries. Knowing what kind of goals to set is a crucial step in getting started. Once you've begun, Chapter 5 will help you organize your efforts and create action teams and work groups to get the job done.

Chapter 6 provides everything you need to conduct inservices on Tech Prep, including suggestions on how to give presentations and who to give them to, as well as transparency masters. Chapter 7 explains how to make needed curriculum changes and create a more interactive, integrated, and applied learning environment for students. Chapter 8 outlines the first steps to involve businesses in your efforts. Chapter 9 helps you build a campaign to promote your program. Finally, Chapter 10 helps you find out if your efforts are making a difference and how to measure your successes.

We have provided several additional resources for your use. Resource A includes basic definitions for getting started. Resource B helps identify the core proficiencies used in your own consortium. Resource C is a checklist to help you monitor your progress. A Bibliography, with a list of sources of additional information, is also provided.

Please treat this manual as a starting point. Seek out other educators who are involved in Tech Prep programs. Listen to futurists talk about tomorrow, and keep track of the demographic changes the United States is undergoing. Good luck and keep in touch.

1

Need for Tech Prep

If Horace Mann were to walk the halls of a typical 20th century school, he would feel at home among the paper, pencils, chalkboards, and textbooks. He would quickly recognize students recalling facts from short-term memory, a curriculum segregated into separate subjects, standardized tests, and teachers being "the sage on the stage" pouring facts into empty vessels. On the other hand, if Horace Mann were to visit a modern business or organization, he would probably feel lost among the technology and workplace climate. Schools are in a precarious position because they have not kept pace with workplace changes. While organizations and businesses have been going through a metamorphosis, education is still mired in 19th-century curriculum and instruction patterns.

School leaders must create change within the education system. The United States must produce graduates who can perform effectively in the changing workplace. In order to do this, we must understand recent trends in the workplace. Only then can we begin to build a system that will accomplish our goal. Not only must leadership be evident at all levels of the education system, but cooperation must exist among these levels. Primary, secondary, and postsecondary schools must work cooperatively to accomplish the goal of producing a workforce for today and tomorrow. Tech Prep is a program that links secondary education, postsecondary education, and the workplace. Tech Prep presents students with a path-

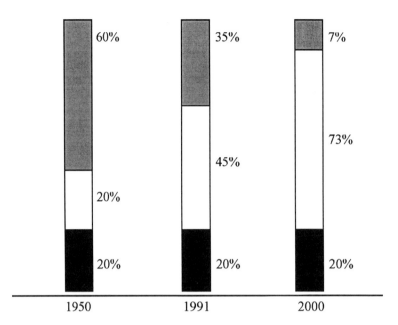

Chart 1.1. Job Skill Level Changes
SOURCE: U.S. Bureau of Labor Statistics.

way to their future. It is an exciting change that is affecting students all over the United States.

Changes in the Workplace

Several changes in the workplace have created a need for school reform. One change is an increase in workplace technology, coupled with the growth of mid-level technical careers. A second change is a shift in the level of education required. Finally, the third change is a shift in the role of the employee.

Workplace Technology and
Growing Mid-Level Technical Careers

The workplace has shifted from unskilled to skilled employment. Chart 1.1 illustrates this shift over time.

Three conclusions are clear from the chart on Job Skill Level Changes:

1. The percentage of unskilled jobs is decreasing
2. The percentage of skilled jobs is increasing
3. The percentage of professional jobs is remaining constant

The shift from unskilled to skilled jobs is primarily a result of the increasing use of technology in the workplace. Every employment sector has been affected by this shift. Examples of the shift from unskilled to skilled jobs are identified below.

- Agriculture has moved from the plow to hydroponics and bioengineered foods
- Manufacturing has shifted from manual labor to robotics
- Service has shifted from a "paper-packed" workplace to a computer-driven environment

Jobs in every sector of the labor market are being shifted from unskilled to skilled by the influx of technology. As this shift occurs, the need for technical education increases.

Level of Education Required for Work

The United States Department of Labor, Bureau of Labor Statistics, released new occupational projections and training data in January 1996. Chart 1.2 summarizes the new category system now being used to report data on employment and level of education.

The chart provides a snapshot of the number of people employed in the occupations studied, the number of occupations available, and the level of education required for each. Four important observations should be noted from the data.

1. Fifty six percent of the occupations require training beyond high school but less than a 4 year degree
2. Only 22% of the occupations require a 4 year degree or more
3. More people are employed in the jobs that require training beyond high school but less than a 4 year degree than in any other category
4. Four out of every 10 jobs will be filled at the lowest level of training (a few days of on-the-job training); however, these are also the lowest paying jobs

These data do not support the traditional belief that all students need a 4 year college degree. The data do indicate that students need some post-high school training to obtain employment. Although

NUMBER OF OCCUPATIONS	NUMBER OF PEOPLE EMPLOYED	LEVEL OF EDUCATION
6	1.0	DOCTORATE
10	1.4	MASTERS
16	2.4	PROFESSIONAL
8	1.7	BACHELOR + 2 YRS
14	8.1	BACHELOR + WORK EXP
64	13.9	BACHELOR
16	4.0	ASSOCIATE
29	7.2	POSTSECONDARY
39	9.9	RELATED WORK EXPER
89	13.7	> 12 MONTHS OJT
119	16.2	1-12 MONTHS OJT
120	49.7	FEW DAYS OJT

Chart 1.2. Employment Data
SOURCE: U.S. Department of Labor.

these data focus on current occupations, the new projections for the fastest growing occupations and the occupations with the largest numerical increases are also available. These data are in Charts 1.3 and 1.4.

The Changing Role of the Employee

The third shift occurring in the workplace focuses on the role of the employee. Organizations now expect workers to be active members of the workplace. Techniques like total quality management require that employees be directly involved in solving the problems of the workplace. Employees are expected to "bring their brains to work" rather than "checking them at the door."

The skills today's workers need were identified in 1988 in a report titled *Workplace Basics: The Skills Employers Want*. These skills are identified in Box 1.1.

Another important publication produced in 1991 by the Secretary's Commission on Achieving Necessary Skills (SCANS) called for teaching the same types of skills. The SCANS report recommended a three-part foundation of skills as well as five competencies. These recommendations appear below.

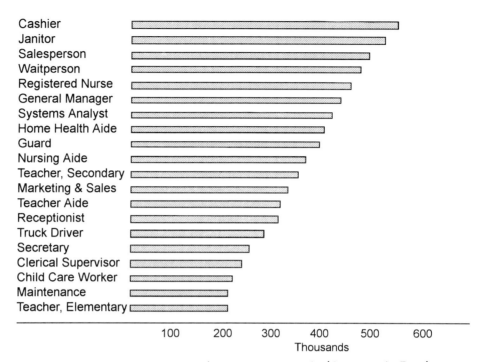

Chart 1.3. Occupations Having the Largest Numerical Increase in Employment, 1994-2005
SOURCE: U.S. Department of Labor.

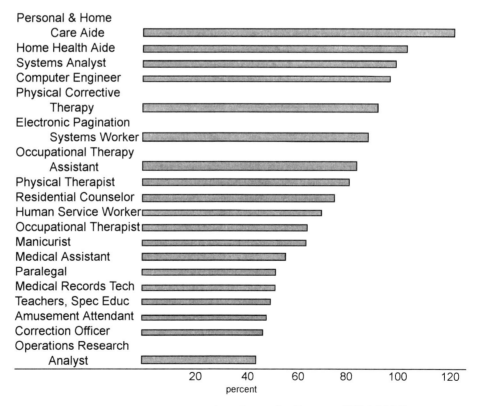

Chart 1.4. Occupations Projected to Grow the Fastest, 1994-2005
SOURCE: U.S. Department of Labor.

BOX 1.1
New Basic Skills

Learning to Learn
Reading, Writing, Computation
Listening and Oral Communication
Creative Thinking/Problem Solving
Personal and Career Development
Negotiation and Teamwork
Organizational Effectiveness

SOURCE: Adapted from *Workplace Basics: The Skills Employers Want*, Carnevale, Gainer, and Meltzer, © copyright 1988 by U.S. Department of Labor, Employment and Training Administration. Reprinted with permission.

SCANS, SKILLS, AND COMPETENCIES

A Three-Part Foundation

Basic Skills

Reads, writes, performs arithmetic and mathematical operations, listens, and speaks

Thinking Skills

Thinks creatively, makes decisions, solves problems, visualizes, knows how to learn, and reasons

Personal Qualities

Displays responsibility, self-esteem, sociability, self-management, integrity and honesty

Five Competencies

Resources

Time, money, material and facilities, human

Interpersonal

Team, teaching, serve clients, leadership, negotiates, works with diversity

Information

Acquires and evaluates, organizes and maintains, interprets and communicates, uses computers to process.

HIGH SCHOOL COURSES	POST HIGH SCHOOL GOAL
COLLEGE PREPARATORY	FOUR YEAR UNIVERSITY/COLLEGE
VOCATIONAL EDUCATION	EMPLOYMENT
GENERAL EDUCATION*	**?**

* These students are often referred to as the neglected majority.

Chart 1.5. The Current Focus of Education
SOURCE: Adapted from *Tech Prep Associate Degree: A Win/Win Experience*, Hull and Parnell, © copyright 1991 by CORD Communications. Reprinted with permission.
NOTE: The term "the neglected majority" comes from Dale Parnell, *The Neglected Majority* (Washington, DC: The Community College Press, 1985).

Systems

Understands, monitors, and corrects performance, improves or designs

Technology

Selects, applies, maintains, and troubleshoots

SOURCE: Adapted from *What Work Requires of Schools: A SCANS Report for America 2000*, Secretary's Commission on Achieving Necessary Skills, © copyright 1991 by U.S. Department of Labor. Reprinted with permission.

The Current Focus of Education

If we are to respond to the changing workplace, we must do two things: produce more qualified workers and educate all students. To do this, we must change the status quo. Chart 1.5 is a diagram illustrating the current system of education at many high schools.

The Tracks in Education

Most educators are familiar with the three "tracks" in Chart 1.5, but they often deny that such "tracks" exist within their own school. There is usually a definite sequence of courses suggested for college preparatory and vocational students. General education students, however, typically drift along without direction.

Students who enroll in college preparatory courses are well equipped to enter a 4 year college or university. These students

> *Regardless of which high school course sequence a student takes, he or she is at a disadvantage in the job market and the workplace. "College preparatory" students lack specific skill knowledge, "vocational students" lack the theoretical foundations and the requirements for promotion, and "general education" students lack specific skill knowledge needed for promotion as well as the theoretical foundations of subject areas.*

usually have no skill training because their curriculum includes an emphasis on theory rather than application.

Students who enroll in vocational courses are well equipped to enter the workforce in a specific career. The curriculum in the vocational courses focuses on the application of content rather than theoretical foundations. Vocational students are able to obtain employment; however, they often must return to education to receive a degree and advance their career.

Students who enroll in general education courses are not equipped to enter a 4 year college/university, nor are they able to obtain work in a "skilled" position. These students do not receive skill training or theoretical foundations within the curriculum. They see little relevance to their education and are therefore not motivated to perform.

What Happens to High School Graduates?

It is estimated that approximately half of all high school graduates enroll in a 4 year degree program immediately after high school. Chart 1.6 illustrates specifically what happens to students in the years following high school.

How Tech Prep Can Make a Difference

Tech Prep is a program that responds to the changing needs of the workplace. It prepares students to use technology and work in the growing number of mid-level technical careers. Tech Prep focuses students toward a 2 year degree or certificate, and it provides training in workplace skills.

Tradition vs. Tech Prep

Chart 1.7 offers a comparison between the traditional classroom and a Tech Prep classroom.

What Happens to High School Graduates?**

1980   55% Entered a four year College/University
               45% Did not enter college

1982   31% Were still enrolled in college
               67% Were not enrolled in college

1987   24% Received a Bachelor's degree
              8% Arts & Sciences
           16% Professional Fields
        76% Did not receive a degree

                             ** Longitudinal study by ETS.

Chart 1.6. What Happens to High School Graduates?
SOURCE: Adapted from *Performance at the Top: From Elementary Through Graduate School,* Policy Information Center, Educational Testing Service, © copyright 1991 by Educational Testing Service. Reprinted with permission.

TRADITIONAL CLASSROOM	TECH PREP CLASSROOM
Courses selected at random	Courses selected from sequence of courses
Teacher plays a "Sage on the stage"	Teacher plays a facilitator for students
Courses are presented as stand alone	Courses are integrated with many subjects
Workplace skills are not covered	Workplace skills are within the curriculum
Students have little or no career focus	Students select a career cluster to pursue
Teachers work in isolation	Teachers work in teams

Chart 1.7.

Tech Prep is a program that puts many pieces of the reform puzzle together. It allows students to take challenging coursework, encourages teachers to use applied and integrated teaching strategies, provides a smooth transition to postsecondary education programs, and allows all students to benefit from these changes.

Tech Prep can create as much or as little reform as you make happen. This manual will help you create a Tech Prep program designed for your students, teachers, staff, community, and businesses.

A Local Perspective on Tech Prep

The school districts within the Tech Prep Associate Degree Consortium of Johnson/Douglas Counties have been working on Tech Prep for 5 years and are observing the following changes:

- Increased student motivation
- Increased teacher motivation
- Supportive parents and media
- Raised self-concept in students
- Higher expectations of students
- Higher academic performance of students

Bibliography

Carnevale, Anthony P., Gainer, Leila J., & Meltzer, Ann S. (1988). *Workplace basics: The skills employers want.* Washington, DC: U.S. Department of Labor, Employment and Training Administration.

Hull, Dan, & Parnell, Dale. (1991). *Tech Prep associate degree: A win\win experience.* Waco, TX: CORD Communications.

Parnell, Dale. (1985). *The neglected majority.* Washington, DC: The Community College Press.

Policy Information Center, Educational Testing Service. (1991). *Performance at the top: From elementary through graduate school.* Princeton, NJ: Author.

Secretary's Commission on Achieving Necessary Skills. (1991). *What work requires of schools: A SCANS report for America 2000.* Washington, DC: U.S. Department of Labor.

U.S. Department of Labor, Bureau of Labor Statistics. (1996, January). *Occupational projections and training data* (Bulletin 2471). Washington, DC: Author.

U.S. Department of Labor, Bureau of Labor Statistics. (1996, February). *Occupational outlook handbook: 1996-1997 edition* (Bulletin 2470). Washington, DC: Author.

2

How the Program Works

The Components of a Tech Prep Program

If you asked seven different people what a Tech Prep program is, you might receive seven different answers. Despite this, there are some components that appear consistently in Tech Prep programs. The components listed below and discussed in the following pages provide a detailed definition of a Tech Prep program.

1. Course sequences
2. Course sequences built around careers or career clusters
3. Three levels of proficiencies (core, technical, and specialty)
4. High school and postsecondary curriculum
5. Application-based teaching strategies
6. Integration of disciplines and subjects
7. Involvement of business and industry

Tech Prep Programs Build Sequences of Courses

The Tech Prep course sequence begins in high school and extends into postsecondary education. Typically, the sequence begins in grade 9 and extends through grade 14. Both academic and technical courses are included in the sequence required of Tech Prep students.

```
┌─────────────────────────────┐
│  Technical Proficiencies    │
│     (Postsecondary)         │
└─────────────────────────────┘
┌───────────────────────────────────┐
│     Technical Proficiencies       │
│  (High School & Postsecondary)    │
└───────────────────────────────────┘
┌─────────────────────────────────────────┐
│                                           │
│          Core Proficiencies               │
│            (High School)                  │
│                                           │
└─────────────────────────────────────────┘
```

Chart 2.1.
SOURCE: Adapted from *Tech Prep Associate Degree: A Win/Win Experience*, Hull and Parnell, © copyright 1991 by CORD Communications. Reprinted with permission.

Course Sequences Are Built Around Career Clusters

A career cluster usually includes a variety of related occupations. Typical career clusters found in Tech Prep programs include Engineering Technology, Health Services, Business and Information Technology, Human Services, Industrial Technology, and Agricultural Technology. Career clusters should be identified based on labor market trends. Tech Prep programs should build education programs in career clusters that show growth patterns in the employment market.

Tech Prep Programs Typically Are Built Around Three Levels of Proficiencies

These proficiencies are taught across the high school, technical school, and college curriculum. Level 1 consists of core proficiencies, Level 2 consists of technical proficiencies, and Level 3 consists of specialty proficiencies. Chart 2.1 illustrates these proficiency levels.

Level 1: Core Proficiencies

The first set of proficiencies typically is taught in high school. Some people consider these proficiencies the "basic skills" for tomorrow's workplace. The core proficiencies include mathematics, science, communication, and technology. Some Tech Prep programs, however, add workplace and career development proficiencies to this list. All Tech Prep students focus on the same core proficiencies regardless of the career or career cluster they are interested in.

Level 2: Technical Proficiencies

The second set of proficiencies can be taught at the high school, technical school, or college level. Where these proficiencies are taught will depend on the technical programs available within your consortium schools. Technical proficiencies introduce students to a career area by providing introductory skill instruction. For example, students interested in an engineering career might attain technical proficiencies in drafting or electronics at this level of the program. Students interested in a career in business might attain technical proficiencies in computer applications at this level. This is usually the first opportunity students have to explore specific careers without having to make a commitment to one particular career.

Level 3: Specialty Proficiencies

The third set of proficiencies is taught at the technical school or college level. Specialty proficiencies provide the students skill training for an occupation. For example, at this level engineering students attain skills in advanced computer-aided drafting and design. Students in a business cluster work on advanced office management proficiencies at this level. These courses provide the specific skills needed for entrance into the workforce.

High School and Postsecondary Curriculum

The three proficiency levels are taught within courses across high school and postsecondary institutions. The core proficiencies are taught at the high school. Technical proficiencies are taught at the high school and/or at a technical school. The specialty proficiencies are covered at the postsecondary level. Coordination between the high school and postsecondary school is essential to ensure that courses are not duplicated and that students have the necessary skills to enter the program at the postsecondary level.

Application-Based Teaching Strategies

Tech Prep programs build curriculum around the integration of academic and technical learning. When academic and technical courses are integrated, students see connections between the class-room and the world of work. Students in math class, for example, learn how the skills they are learning are used on the job. Coordi-nation between the high school and postsecondary school is essen-tial to ensure that courses are not duplicated and that students have the prerequisite skills to enter the program at the postsecondary level.

Integration of Disciplines and Subjects

A Tech Prep curriculum builds strong ties among disciplines and subjects. Two specific integration levels are stressed in Tech Prep programs. First, students must understand how components within subject areas are related to one another. For example, how are chemistry, physics, and biology related? How is algebra related to geometry and statistics? Second, students must understand how disciplines are related to one another. Here we refer to the relation-ships between physics and music, or between science and mathe-matics. Tech Prep students leave high school with one large box that contains knowledge and skills rather than separate boxes with labels such as geometry, biology, and language arts.

Involvement of Business and Industry

One of the major goals of Tech Prep is to increase linkages between education and business. Involving business and industry representatives in the Tech Prep program is important to building a strong, work-based curriculum. Business representatives can be involved in Tech Prep in a variety of ways.

How a Tech Prep Program Will Help Students

Most Tech Prep programs have just begun to collect data on the impact of Tech Prep. Tech Prep practitioners often cite the following benefits as arising, at least in part, from their Tech Prep programs. Tech Prep programs are designed to do the following.

1. Raise the Academic Performance Levels of Students in Mathematics, English, Technology, and Science

Many students stop taking math and science courses in their sophomore year of high school, and most students never take technology-related courses at all. By encouraging or requiring stu-dents to enroll in more math, science, and technology courses and by teaching those courses using application teaching strategies, we can raise their academic performance.

2. Increase Student Motivation to Learn

Tech Prep courses present concepts by grounding them in workplace application. When students begin to understand how mathematics, for example, is used outside the classroom, they stop asking, "When am I ever going to use this?" and become involved in learning.

3. Connect High School With College by Providing a Coordinated Sequence of Courses

Tech Prep programs build sequences of courses that begin in high school and culminate with a 2 year postsecondary degree or certificate. These sequences provide a smooth transition for students from high school to college and ensure that coursework is not duplicative. When programs are coordinated in this manner, students are prepared for the next level of education.

4. Decrease Dropout Rates of High School Students

Tech Prep programs, when used to replace the "general education" program, can help to reduce the number of high school dropouts. The Tech Prep program provides direction and challenge that students often do not have in the "general education" program.

5. Increase Students' Preparedness to Enter College Degree Programs

As Tech Prep program students progress through the recommended sequence of courses, they will attain high levels of mathematics, science, and technology skills. Because the course sequence has been designed jointly by high school and college faculty, students are well prepared to enter postsecondary programs. Tech Prep students will bypass the remedial courses offered in many postsecondary institutions.

6. Increase Skill Levels of Graduates

As Tech Prep students enter the postsecondary portion of the program, they will be entering with high levels of math, science, and technology skills. The postsecondary institutions may then raise the content levels of their programs. Raising the content covered in postsecondary degree programs will allow students to attain higher skill levels at the completion of the program.

7. Provide Age-Appropriate
School-to-Work Transition Activities

Involving business and industry representatives in the Tech Prep program will help students stay closely related to their career interests. Students should have the opportunity to investigate and explore various careers as they move from junior high or middle school to high school and on into postsecondary education.

8. Provide Information on Career Opportunities
for Community College Graduates

The Tech Prep program focuses attention on careers of the future and the skills necessary to succeed in them. Research predicts that 80% of future new jobs will require less than a bachelor's degree. Providing current career and labor market information helps students and parents make appropriate career decisions.

Making Tech Prep Work

Consortium Commitment

All consortium members must be committed to building a Tech Prep program. Everyone is important to making the Tech Prep program work. Gaining active support for the program from all participants is a key element in the program's success.

Administrative Commitment

The commitment to a Tech Prep program at the administrative level is one of the most important pieces of an effective program. Faculty and staff members will not be able to make the changes required by the program if administrators and board members are not solidly behind the changes.

Persistence

The Tech Prep program will not appear overnight; in fact, if it does, you should be suspicious. Typically, faculty members and counselors must first believe that change is needed. The changes made within a Tech Prep program are complex and cannot be made all at once. The easiest way to approach the changes is to identify a small task and work on accomplishing that one task. Once the first small task has been accomplished, you can carve out the next task.

Resources

Several kinds of resources will be needed to implement a Tech Prep program. These resources include planning time, funding to support equipment needs, in-service programs, and time to meet with faculty from the postsecondary level.

Essential Roles in a Tech Prep Program

It is essential to have many people involved in a Tech Prep program. The following section suggests specific roles for some personnel within a Tech Prep program. This is not a comprehensive list of roles. For organizational purposes, we have divided these roles into consortium, secondary, and postsecondary categories.

Consortium Roles

Coordinator/Director

The Tech Prep director focuses on organizing and coordinating the consortium activities. A common mistake is for a consortium to hire a director and believe that the director will create the program. It is impossible for the director to implement Tech Prep alone. The director cannot create change within each school; that must be done by local school personnel.

Secondary Roles

Superintendent/Assistant Superintendent

The superintendent may serve on the steering committee (chapter 3) and provide visibility for the program within the home district. This might be done by keeping the school board and community informed and involved with Tech Prep efforts. The superintendent should also stay in communication with other Tech Prep consortium administrators.

Curriculum Director

The curriculum director should serve a major role in the development of Tech Prep at the local level. This person should also serve on the curriculum work team. It would be helpful to have this person serve as chairperson of the action team.

Principal

The principal should provide leadership within the high school to keep Tech Prep efforts moving. The principal may serve as chairperson of the building team and as a member of the district action team (chapter 5). Providing support for teachers who work on curriculum or articulation is also important for the principal. Encouraging teachers and staff to be creative and supporting that creativity with funding (if necessary) is crucial to making the program work.

Teachers

Teachers serve as members of the district action team and the building team. In this capacity, they should plan the district/building efforts for Tech Prep. It is also important for these teachers to reach out to other teachers to get them involved in the program.

Counselors

Counselors must serve as "recruiters" for the Tech Prep program. Because counselors control the enrollment in classes, they must support the curriculum changes being made. Counselors also can provide some career development to students; however, they should not be responsible for an entire career development program for Tech Prep. A career development program requires involvement of the entire staff, not just the counselors.

Postsecondary Roles

President/Vice President

The president or vice president (depending on the size of the school) should provide visibility for the program at the postsecondary level as well as to the board of trustees and the community. Involvement at this level is often perceived as a sign of the total commitment of an institution.

Dean of Instruction

The dean of instruction (again depending on the size of the school) should serve on the steering committee (chapter 3) and provide direction to the program. This person might serve as the force behind the changes on the postsecondary level. There are many policy and procedural decisions to be made regarding such matters as the granting of college credit. It is helpful if this person is a champion for Tech Prep at the postsecondary level.

Teachers

Postsecondary teachers might serve on articulation teams or curriculum integration teams (chapter 5). It is helpful if these teachers reach out to secondary school teachers to build a bridge across the institutions.

Use *The Essential Roles Checklist* below to determine how well your consortium is moving along.

1. Does the consortium have a director/coordinator?
2. Is the director/coordinator acting as an organizer of the consortium activities?
3. Is there someone in a district-level position creating visibility for Tech Prep?
4. Is there administrative leadership for Tech Prep in each high school?
5. Is there someone at the postsecondary level (other than the Tech Prep director) creating visibility for Tech Prep?
6. Is there someone handling the policy/procedural issues at the postsecondary level (other than the Tech Prep director)?

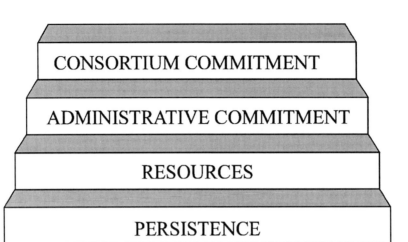

CONSORTIUM COMMITMENT

All consortium members must be actively committed to building a Tech Prep program. *Commitment is important to making the Tech Prep program work.*

ADMINISTRATIVE COMMITMENT

The commitment to a Tech Prep program at the administrative level is vital to building an effective program. Faculty and staff members will not be able to make the changes required by the program if administrators and board members are not solidly behind the changes.

RESOURCES

Several types of resources will be needed to implement a Tech Prep program. These resources include: planning time, funding to support equipment needs, inservice programs, and time for faculty to work on curriculum.

PERSISTENCE

The Tech Prep program will not appear overnight; in fact, if it does, you should be suspicious. Typically, faculty members and counselors must first believe that change is needed. Changes made to implement a Tech Prep program are complex and cannot be carried out all at once. Identify the steps to be accomplished and focus on a few steps at a time. Once the first few steps have been accomplished, you can carve out the next task.

Chart 2.2. What Does it Take to Make Tech Prep Work?

3

Creating the Tech Prep Consortium

What Is a Tech Prep Consortium?

In general, a consortium is a group of individuals joined together in partnership to accomplish a specific task. A Tech Prep consortium is a group of schools brought together to develop and implement a Tech Prep program. The very nature of Tech Prep requires that a consortium be created to develop the program. Because the program joins high schools with postsecondary schools, it is impossible to create a Tech Prep program without at least one high school and one postsecondary school (community college, technical school, college, or university).

The primary members of a Tech Prep consortium are schools, however, some Tech Prep programs also seek to involve businesses at an integral level. If this is part of the goal for your Tech Prep program, you may want to consider making some area businesses members of your consortium.

The Functions of a Tech Prep Consortium

A consortium can perform many different functions for its members. Specific functions can and should be defined locally to fit the needs of each consortium. We recommend that you clearly identify the

Why Is a Consortium Important in Tech Prep?

A Tech Prep program involves both high school (secondary) and college (postsecondary) education, so it is impossible to develop a Tech Prep program without a consortium. The more schools you involve in the consortium, the greater the potential for interaction among teachers, staff members, and administrators.

functions your consortium will perform. This prevents any misunderstandings about the role of the consortium staff. Below are examples of functions typically performed by the Tech Prep consortium.

1. Provide linkages among consortium members.
2. Provide in-service programs to consortium members.
3. Identify tomorrow's career opportunities.
4. Structure career clusters.
5. Assist schools in producing promotional messages.

Provide Linkages Among Consortium Members

There are two important components involved in providing linkages. The first is the set of linkages between each of the high schools and the postsecondary institution (see Chart 3.1). Each high school will need to have a working relationship with the postsecondary institution in order to build a smooth transition from high school to college.

The second link should be among the different high schools in the consortium (see Chart 3.2). One of the greatest advantages of working in a consortium is the opportunity to collaborate with teachers, counselors, and administrators from other schools. Having the opportunity to see what other teachers are doing with similar classes can be valuable in making changes in our own classes. Educators at all levels are isolated from one another. The consortium offers an opportunity to interact and exchange ideas in a nonthreatening environment.

Provide In-Service Programs to Consortium Members

The consortium staff can provide some of the in-service programs that will be needed to get the program started. Typically, the

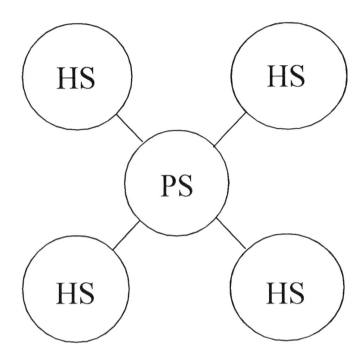

HS = High School
PS = Postsecondary

Chart 3.1.

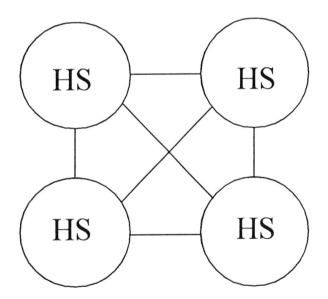

HS = High School

Chart 3.2.

introductory programs on Tech Prep include topics such as What is Tech Prep?, Why is Tech Prep needed?, and What are the components of a Tech Prep program? All of these topics should be within the consortium director's knowledge base and ability. Additional in-service programs can be arranged by the consortium by hiring consultants to provide programs in needed topic areas.

Identify Tomorrow's Career Opportunities

The consortium staff should have access to current labor market information. The U.S. Department of Labor publishes occupational projections as well as a journal titled *Occupational Outlook Quarterly*. It is important for members of the consortium to understand what is happening in today's employment marketplace. The consortium should provide the information to teachers, counselors, parents, students, and business and community members. The more your consortium and community members know about the changing labor market, the more effective the program will be.

Structure the Career Clusters

The consortium may also determine which career clusters become a part of the program. A career cluster is a group of careers or occupations for which training is available at the postsecondary level. The careers are related to the main cluster title, though not necessarily to one another. Examples of career clusters include:

Engineering Technology Cluster
Drafting Technology
Electronics Technology
Civil Engineering Technology
Communications Technology
Industrial Technology Cluster
Automotive Technology
Metal Fabrication
Railroad Operations
Heating, Ventilation, and Air Conditioning
Health Technology Cluster
Radiologic Technology
Dental Hygiene
Emergency Medical Science
Nursing
Respiratory Care

> **Human Services Cluster**
> Fire Science
> Criminal Justice
> Cosmetology
> **Information Technology Cluster**
> Data Processing
> Commercial Art
> **Business Technology Cluster**
> Office Systems Technology
> Accounting
> Marketing/Management
> Paralegal
> Tele-Service

Assist Schools in Producing Promotional Messages

Local schools may not have the resources to produce promotional materials for the program. A consortium can create a few promotional pieces that all schools can use and some pieces that can be customized for local schools. For example, a videotape, radio spots, and media events are all products the consortium might consider creating for local schools. Individual schools may be able to produce their own press releases and articles for local newspapers and magazines.

Forming a Tech Prep Consortium

Almost any group of schools can form a consortium. The minimum requirements for a Tech Prep consortium are one secondary and one postsecondary school. Here are a few simple steps which can be followed to set up your consortium. As you work through these steps, remember that your consortium should fit your local needs.

1. Assess interest in forming a Tech Prep consortium.
2. Create the consortium.

Assess Interest in Forming a Tech Prep Consortium

The first meeting held should be attended by the chief school officer from each institution. The superintendent is the secondary school representative who usually participates at this first meeting. The president or vice president for academic affairs is often the postsecondary school representative. During this first meeting, you should create a basic understanding of what a Tech Prep program is, what a Tech Prep consortium is, and how the consortium can function, as well as determining who is interested in creating the consortium.

At the conclusion of the first meeting, it should be clear which parties are interested in participating in developing the program. Once you know who is interested in participating in the Tech Prep consortium, you can conduct a second meeting in which you work through the steps of creating the consortium.

Create the Consortium

Creating the consortium involves establishing some organizational rules and expectations. The second meeting should include the same chief school officers who attended the first meeting and should add another key person from each institution. Usually this second person is the one who ultimately will be responsible for implementing the program in the school.

This second meeting should cover the following topics:

1. Identify conditions for consortium membership.
2. Identify the functions the consortium will serve.
3. Form a steering committee.
4. Identify sources of funding.
5. Develop a formal statement of agreement.

Identify Conditions for Consortium Membership

Identifying conditions for consortium membership is a process of creating minimum expectations for consortium members. Consortia can be built as tight or relaxed organizations. It is important that you design the consortium as it will be most effective for your local situation. It is helpful, however, to lay out expectations of each consortium member before entering into the project. This way, members know the tasks to be accomplished. Some of the issues you may want to address are identified below.

Minimum Length of Commitment for Members. Will each member be required to make a minimum time commitment to the project? Typically, significant change takes a minimum of 5 years to occur. You may want to consider asking members to agree to a minimum of 3 years in the original agreement.

Minimum Activities for Members. You may want to set minimum activities for members. For example, members should develop at least one career cluster, participate in consortiumwide in-service programs, and provide district representation to consortium work teams.

Local Funding Commitment. Will each member be required to make some sort of financial commitment to the project? This may take the form of funds for equipment, or it may be in curriculum development in-service time, substitute days, or overload hours.

Identify the Functions the Consortium Will Serve for Its Members

Identifying the consortium functions will help members understand the role each member plays in the development of the program. The functions discussed in the previous section can be used as a guide to select the functions your consortium will provide.

Form a Steering Committee

The next step is to form one main steering committee. The purpose of this committee is to provide the vision/mission for Tech Prep and to organize the work involved in creating the Tech Prep program. Each consortium member should designate at least one person to serve on the steering committee.

Hull and Parnell (1991) suggest creating two different committees for this function. The leadership and implementation committees (described below) could be combined into one group that makes the final decisions and serves as the "workhorse" for the project. It is not important how many committees you create for the steering of the project, as long as the tasks get accomplished.

Leadership Committee. The primary purpose of this committee is to commit the institutions in the consortium to a Tech Prep program and make that commitment visible. The committee has overall responsibility for the program and makes final decisions.

Implementation Committee. This committee has been referred to as the "workhorse" of all the committees. It is responsible for making the major decisions that go into formal agreements and for establishing the other committees that report back to it.

We suggest that the following kinds of people might serve on the steering committee(s): the director of secondary education, technical managers, the principal or vice principal, human relations directors, the associate superintendent, program directors, department chairpersons, and deans/assistant deans.

The steering committee might serve the following specific functions:

1. Create and appoint any additional committees/teams to work on the Tech Prep project.
2. Address and finalize consortiumwide issues as they arise in curriculum development, promotion/information, evaluation/assessment, and business and industry involvement.
3. Be responsible for Tech Prep within each school or organization.

The steering committee does not need to have specific knowledge within all three areas identified above. The committee must call on specific people to meet and make recommendations in each of the areas listed above. The steering committee's role is to finalize decisions, not necessarily to do all the work involved in investigating the problems and seeking solutions. In Tech Prep, value lies in tapping expertise outside the steering committee and consortium staff. The steering committee's role is to finalize decisions. It is not responsible for all the work involved in creating a Tech Prep program.

Identify Sources of Funding

Another question consortium members should discuss is how the consortium will be funded. There are several sources of funding available for Tech Prep programs. Some of these sources are identified below.

State Funding. Several states have appropriated funds to support the development of Tech Prep programs. We recommend that you contact your state education department or agency for additional information on this source of funding.

Federal Funding. Although federal legislation is currently in flux, there are some sources for federal funding. The current Carl Perkins Vocational and Applied Technology Education Act is the major source of federal funding for Tech Prep. This legislation contains two sources of support for Tech Prep. You should look at using program improvement money from Title II or the competitive dollars from Title III. You should contact your state department of education or the agency in your state that handles Carl Perkins funding.

The School to Work Opportunities Act also supports the kinds of activities included in a Tech Prep program. The school-to-work emphasis, however, is an even more systemic change than Tech Prep. The new block grant being discussed now will support the same kinds of activities that Tech Prep supports. Specifics are not available, as the legislation is not final.

Local Funding. One should never overlook the obvious. Schools already allocate funds for curriculum development and in-service programs. If Tech Prep is a district priority, local money can be reallocated within the district.

How much money does it take to implement Tech Prep? We are confident that there is no one set amount of money it takes to implement Tech Prep. We suspect that it takes as much money as is available in the budget! The minimum expenditure we recommend is the hiring of a person (director or coordinator) who can focus efforts on the project. When the project is assigned to someone who already has a full-time job, it often gets lost in the shuffle.

There may be some equipment needed to implement applied teaching strategies in the classroom; however, we see no need for expensive purchases, especially early in the development of the program. The kinds of manipulatives needed for applied teaching strategies often can be purchased from local department stores. We are always encouraged by teachers who find innovative ways to teach in an applied fashion for very little money. If a school decides to implement an expensive program, this decision should be made carefully and over a reasonable amount of time. Purchases of pre-packaged curriculum and equipment should be made with care.

In addition to determining the sources of funding, it is important to agree on the activities to be funded. The following is a list of activities typically found within a Tech Prep program budget.

- Personnel
  Professional staff: Tech Prep coordinator/director
  Support staff: secretary
- In-Service Needs
  Travel
  Consultants
  Workshop fees
- Curriculum Development
  Curriculum materials
  Substitute pay/stipends
- Instructional Equipment
  Lab materials
- Promotional Items (video, brochures, newsletters, etc.)

Develop a Formal Statement of Agreement

Developing a written agreement is a way for the consortium members to solidify the consortium as an organization. An agreement can be formal and detailed or informal and general. It should be signed by all consortium members. It can be used to promote the project and the commitment of the members.

This is an example of an agreement presented by Hull and Parnell (1991). Unlike the one we used in our own consortium, this one is relatively informal and general.

Executive Articulation Agreement

The institutions listed below are committed to developing and implementing a 2 + 2 secondary/postsecondary Tech Prep program in _____ Technology. The curriculum to be installed will allow a high school student to enroll in classes at the high school that qualify for postsecondary credit after the student has been graduated. The program is to begin by _____.

_____   _____
CEO, Secondary School   CEO, Postsecondary Institution

_____
CEO, Secondary School

The following is an example of a written agreement we used in our own consortium.

Agreement of Participation for the Tech Prep Associate Degree Consortium of Johnson/Douglas Counties

We, the undersigned, agree to participate in the Tech Prep Associate Degree Consortium of Johnson/Douglas Counties from July _____ to July _____.

The objectives listed below are the minimum activities for a member of the consortium.

1. Send representation to consortiumwide committees.

   Each participating member agrees to develop promotional materials and evaluation strategies, provide input from business/industry, develop curriculum, and perform other related activities. Tech Prep funds shall be used to provide substitutes and stipends for staff.

2. Appoint and support the efforts of a local Tech Prep action team.

   Each participating member agrees to establish and support a local action team in the design of a sequence of courses that fulfills the core proficiencies and one of the Tech Prep clusters.

3. Promote the concept of Tech Prep within the local school and community.

   Each participating member agrees to promote the idea of Tech Prep as a viable option for students.

_____   _____

_____   _____

_____   _____

_____   _____

_____   _____

The Consortium Worksheet

Use this worksheet to form your consortium.

1. List Tech Prep consortium members.

_____

_____

_____

_____

_____

2. Identify any conditions for consortium membership.

_____

_____

_____

_____

_____

3. Identify the funding source(s) for the consortium and the activities to be funded.

_____

_____

_____

_____

_____

The Consortium Worksheet, Continued

4. Identify the functions the consortium will serve.

_____

_____

_____

_____

_____

5. Identify items to be included in the formal agreement.

_____

_____

_____

_____

_____

6. List the members of the Tech Prep Consortium Steering Committee.

_____

_____

_____

_____

_____

_____

References

Hull, Dan, & Parnell, Dale. (1991). *Tech Prep associate degree: A win\win experience*. Waco, TX: CORD Communications.

Occupational Outlook Quarterly. Bureau of Labor Statistics.

4

Getting Started

Once the consortium has been formed and the steering committee is in place, the Tech Prep program must be defined. The consortium members must come to consensus regarding the purpose of the program and the specific parameters to be used. Defining the Tech Prep program is the first task for the steering committee to tackle. This can be accomplished by following the steps listed below.

1. Create vision and mission statements.
2. Set parameters for the program.

The first task for the steering committee is to establish a vision and mission for the project. Here are some suggestions for creating the vision and mission:

1. Devote at least one full meeting to developing the vision/mission.
2. Have an outside facilitator run the vision/mission meeting.
3. If a member of the consortium runs the meeting, this person should act as a facilitator and not a participant.

**Tech Prep Associate Degree Consortium
of Johnson/Douglas Counties**

VISION STATEMENT
To implement a nationally recognized Tech Prep program that joins business and education to prepare all students for a rapidly changing workforce through enhancing technical, communication and collaborative skills.

MISSION STATEMENT
To develop and offer **programs of study** in expanding career fields using **innovative teaching methods** that engage and empower students by bringing the workplace and the classroom together.

> **Programs of study**-sequences of courses and learning opportunities offered in high school and college.

> **Innovative teaching methods**-new, nontraditional, and creative teaching procedures that apply learning, integrate subjects and disciplines, and tap a variety of learning styles.

Chart 4.1.

Creating Vision and Mission Statements

What Is a Vision Statement?

A vision statement is a representation of how the program is viewed. The vision statement should be a lofty statement that reaches into the future. The statement will be used to guide the sights of consortium members. Many organizational consultants are available to assist your consortium with writing the vision statement. The consortium should not hesitate to revisit the vision statement and rewrite it now and then. The vision must always be current.

What Is a Mission Statement?

The mission statement describes how the vision will be accomplished. The mission statement should indicate the activities that will take place in order to achieve the vision. Unlike the vision, a mission statement is not lofty but very practical. The mission statement should serve as the overall goal for your Tech Prep program. Chart 4.1 is an example of a vision and mission statement used by the Tech Prep Associate Degree Consortium of Johnson/Douglas Counties.

Setting Parameters for the Program

Selecting a Tech Prep Model

Several Tech Prep models are available for consideration. Each model lays out a slightly different grade-level structure. Here are some examples of Tech Prep models.

2 + 2 Tech Prep Program

A 2 + 2 Tech Prep program includes the last 2 years of high school (Grades 11 and 12) and the first 2 years of postsecondary school (Grades 13 and 14). This model provides for students to earn an associate degree or certificate and lays out a sequence of courses for these 4 years.

4 + 2 Tech Prep Program

A 4 + 2 Tech Prep program begins in the 9th grade of high school and extends through the first 2 years of postsecondary school. This program also provides for students to earn an associate degree or certificate. The course sequence for this program covers 6 years.

2 + 2 + 2 Tech Prep Program

A 2 + 2 + 2 Tech Prep program typically begins in the junior year of high school and includes 2 years of postsecondary school that provide an associate degree, plus an additional 2 years at a 4 year college to complete a bachelor's degree. This program lays out a 6 year sequence of courses culminating with a bachelor's degree.

4 + 2 + 2 Tech Prep Program

A 4 + 2 + 2 Tech Prep program begins in the 9th grade and takes students through the associate degree or certificate and the bachelor's degree. This program lays out an 8 year sequence of courses.

Time-Shortened vs. Advanced Skill Programs

Another important consideration in building your program involves the selection of a time-shortened or an advanced skill

A word of caution is advised in naming a number of years to complete an associate degree program. Many associate degree programs cannot be completed in 2 years. A word of caution is also advised when building a Tech Prep program into the bachelor degree level. Many associate degrees in technical fields do not allow smooth transitions into bachelor's degree programs. We suggest that you discuss specific degree programs with representatives from 4 year colleges and universities before including this feature as a part of your Tech Prep program.

program. It is important to make this decision early in the planning stage of your program so that subsequent decisions are appropriate.

A time-shortened program allows students to obtain advanced standing credit for postsecondary work while they are still in high school. The advanced credit they receive gives them a head start on the postsecondary curriculum and allows completion of the degree sooner. In this scenario, the postsecondary institution does not change its degree programs at all.

An advanced skill program also allows high school students to received advanced standing credit for work completed in high school. This kind of program, however, usually adds additional coursework on the upper end of the degree program so that students leave with more advanced skills. For example, an introduction to drafting course may provide high school students with college credit; however, the credits will satisfy a prerequisite to the degree program rather than a part of the degree program itself. The postsecondary program can take students farther by adding additional skills training.

Tech Prep Definition Worksheet

1. Create a vision for the Tech Prep program.

_____

_____

_____

_____

2. Create a mission statement for the Tech Prep program.

_____

_____

_____

_____

3. What grade levels will your Tech Prep program include?

_____

4. Will this be a time-shortened or an advanced skill program?

_____

_____

_____

5

Organizing the Teams

We recommend organizing the Tech Prep program on three levels: consortium, local school district, and postsecondary school. Each of these levels will have its own set of tasks to perform.

Organizing the Consortium

Work teams should be established by the steering committee to facilitate the many activities required to plan and develop a Tech Prep program. Work teams are responsible for handling issues that relate to all consortium members.

Creating Work Teams

There are several main tasks involved in the development and implementation of a Tech Prep program. Some common consortium work teams include curriculum, evaluation, promotion, and business and industry (see Chart 5.1). The specific function of each of these work teams must be defined by the steering committee.

The steering committee is responsible for appointing the work teams. In addition to establishing the membership, the steering committee should define the specific responsibilities of each consortium work team. This will help the team to focus its efforts and

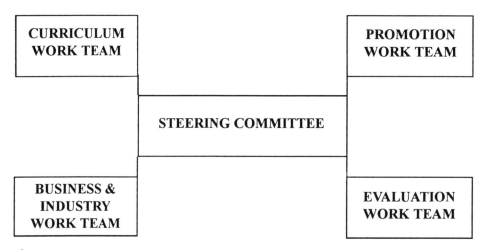

Chart 5.1.

ensure that the team accomplishes what needs to be done. Use the Consortium Work Team Worksheet (page 49) and the sample letter of invitation to serve on a Tech Prep work team (page 50) to help set up the teams.

The steering committee should remember that the work teams are consortium-level teams. As consortium-level teams, their efforts should be focused on issues that affect all members of the consortium. The work teams cannot make decisions for individual schools. Another consideration to keep in mind is that all consortium members should be represented on each of the work teams (unless this creates a very large team). Finally, a chairperson (other than the Tech Prep coordinator) should be appointed for each work team.

The Curriculum Work Team

This work team deals with curriculum policies for the consortium. From our perspective, the curriculum team responds to the following kinds of questions:

- What are the core proficiencies for Tech Prep?
- What are the characteristics of the Tech Prep curriculum?
- What in-service programs must be provided for teachers to shift their teaching strategies?

The team should have the option of creating ad hoc groups to solve specific problems or make recommendations. For example, an ad hoc group might be created to define the core proficiencies for Tech Prep students or build a plan to assist teachers in integrating academic and technical curriculum.

Who Should Serve on the Curriculum Work Team?

The curriculum work team should comprise representatives from each consortium member. It is best to have district-level representation from the secondary schools and administrative-level personnel from the postsecondary schools. Placing only teachers on this work team often does not provide the clout needed to get the job done.

The Promotion Work Team

This work team publicizes the program. If your consortium is large and covers a wide variety of schools (e.g., rural, suburban, large, and small), this team can handle promotion by creating a few major pieces for all consortium members to use. Individual schools can do local promotion for their own initiatives.

Who Should Serve on the Promotion Work Team?

Members of the promotion work team should be from all consortium members. Information directors, media contact people, and other promotion professionals employed by the schools are essential members. Members of the local media also are excellent potential members of this team.

The Evaluation Work Team

This work team assesses the effectiveness of the Tech Prep program. It is important to know if the program is effective. The team must determine what data elements will be collected and analyzed, as well as what kind of conclusions you want to make about the Tech Prep program.

Who Should Serve on the Evaluation Work Team?

Members of the evaluation team should represent all consortium members. You will need people who have knowledge and experience in evaluating programs. It is also important to have people from each school district who handle student data/information.

The Business and Industry Involvement Work Team

This team can plan specific activities to bridge the gap between the skills used on the job and the skills taught within the classroom. Skills such as critical thinking, teamwork, and communication are essential for employees to have and sometimes difficult for teachers to teach within the classroom. Activities such as internships, mentorships, and days on the job can be effective tools in getting the Tech Prep student closer to employment.

*Who Should Serve on the Business
and Industry Involvement Work Team?*

Ideally, this team should be composed primarily of business and industry representatives. Some education personnel are important; however, the driving force for a group like this should be the business community.

When Should the Work Teams Be Created?

We recommend creating the curriculum work team before any of the other teams. This work team must establish the curriculum foundation before other tasks can take place.

When creating a promotion work team, you should be sure you have a program to promote before creating a need in the minds of parents and students.

The evaluation work team can be created early in the project so that data collection procedures are ready when students begin to enroll.

The business and industry involvement work team should be created early in the project. This team can play a crucial role in the development of the program.

Consortium Work Team Worksheet

_____

Name of Work Team

1. List the members below.

_____

_____

_____

_____

_____

_____

2. Identify the goals of the work team.

_____

_____

_____

_____

_____

_____

Dr. Christine Stone
Curriculum Director
Unified School District 111
5647 Pearle Avenue
Overland Park, Kansas 66666

July 1, 1994

Dear Dr. Stone,

The Tech Prep Consortium of Johnson County is building a program to help students prepare for their future. We are building sequences of courses for high school students who want to pursue a two-year degree. We are creating a curriculum work team for the project and would appreciate having you as a member of this team.

The team will handle the major curriculum issues for the schools in the project. The team will be establishing core competencies for students and identifying the curriculum changes to be made within courses. The team will also be designing and implementing an inservice plan to help teachers make the appropriate changes. The team will meet approximately once a month for three hours during this academic year. Specific dates will be set during the first meeting.

The first meeting of the curriculum work team will be on August 23, 1994, at Johnson County Community College. The meeting will begin at 9:00 A.M. in the Cultural Education Center, room 324. Please bring your calendar so we can set subsequent meeting dates. We have enclosed an agenda and a map for your convenience.

If you will be unable to join us on this work team or are unable to make the meeting on August 23, please let us know by contacting the Tech Prep project office at 469-8500, ext. 4143. Thank you for your time and attention.

Warmest regards,

Figure 5.1. Sample Letter of Invitation to Serve on a Tech Prep Work Team

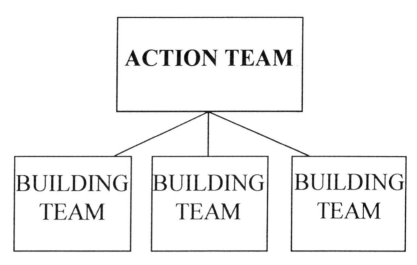

Chart 5.2.

Organizing the Local School District

We have found that it is helpful to have two kinds of Tech Prep teams at the secondary level for implementing the program: an action team and building teams. The local school district is responsible for creating the action and building teams.

Chart 5.2 is a diagram of how a school district with three high schools might be organized for Tech Prep using an action team and building teams.

The following section discusses each of these teams in detail.

Tech Prep Action Teams

The first team we recommend creating is an action team. The action team provides leadership and guides the overall development of the program within the local school district. The district representative to the steering committee should work with the principals to create the action team. Typically, either the steering committee member or a district administrator serves as chairperson of the action team.

The action team should represent all the high schools in the district as well as district-level administrators. High school representatives might include principals, lead teachers, and counselors. District-level representatives might include the superintendent, assistant superintendent, curriculum director, or director of secondary education. A business representative and a board of education member are excellent additions to this group.

The following is a typical list of responsibilities for a Tech Prep action team.

1. Set a district timetable and plan for implementation.
2. Plan in-service activities for faculty and staff.
3. Project budget needs.
4. Promote the Tech Prep program within the community and the school system.
5. Develop/oversee course sequencing and other curriculum changes as necessary.
6. Prepare and present recommendations to the Board of Education.
7. Build agreements with postsecondary schools.
8. Monitor the effectiveness of the Tech Prep program.
9. Involve business and industry representatives in the program.
10. Identify the career clusters to be developed by the district.

Use the worksheet and the sample memorandum of invitation on the next two pages to help create the action team.

Action Team Worksheet

1. Identify the people who will serve on the Action Team.

Name   Position   Building   Phone

_____

_____

_____

_____

_____

_____

_____

_____

_____

_____

_____

_____

_____

_____

_____

MEMORANDUM

TO: Mr. Louis
FROM: Dr. Grant
DATE: August 12, 1994
SUBJECT: Tech Prep Action Team

As you know, our district is involved in the Tech Prep Consortium of Johnson County. We are creating a Tech Prep Action Team for our district and would like to have you as a member of this team. The team will handle district-level decisions about Tech Prep in Olathe.

We will need to meet monthly for the first year. The first meeting has been scheduled for September 16, 1994, at 1:30 P.M. in the conference room at the education center. Please let me know if you will be able to join us on the Tech Prep Action Team.

The agenda for the first meeting is listed below:

  1:30 P.M. Call to order

  1. Introduction of members

  2. Review of Tech Prep Consortium

  3. Goals of the Tech Prep Action Team

  4. Set meeting schedule for the year

  5. Background on Tech Prep Adjournment

Figure 5.2. Sample Memorandum of Invitation to Serve on a Tech Prep Action Team

MEMORANDUM

TO: Ms. Steward
FROM: Dr. Bryant
DATE: September 5, 1994
SUBJECT: Tech Prep Building Team

As you know, our district is involved in the Tech Prep Consortium of Johnson County. We are creating a Tech Prep Building Team for our high school and would like to have you as a member of this team. The team will focus on how Tech Prep will be implemented in our building.

The first meeting has been scheduled for October 4, 1994, at 10:00 A.M. in the library media room. Please let me know if you will be unable to join us for this meeting.

The agenda for the first meeting is listed below:

  10:00 A.M. Call to order

  1. Review of Tech Prep Consortium

  2. Goals of the Tech Prep Building Team

  3. Prioritize goals and assign subteams

Figure 5.3. Sample Memorandum of Invitation to Serve on a Tech Prep Building Team

Tech Prep Building Teams

The second team we recommend creating is a building team within each high school. Tech Prep building teams are responsible for handling implementation issues at the building level. The team should be appointed by the steering committee representative and the principals. This team is best chaired by the principal or other administrator at the building level.

The building team is best composed of the principal, at least one counselor, and at least four teachers from various content areas (academic and technical). A business representative and a board member are excellent additions to this team. Another consideration is to keep common members between the action team and the building teams. You want communication to flow smoothly among these teams.

The following is a typical list of responsibilities for a building team.

1. Assist in developing the curriculum sequence.
2. Promote the program within the high school.
3. Identify and enroll Tech Prep students.
4. Meet with postsecondary school representatives to articulate curriculum.
5. Design and produce recruitment materials for students.
6. Make curriculum changes and work with other faculty and staff toward curriculum changes.

Additional responsibilities should be identified in response to local needs.

The building team will consist of a small portion of the high school staff. It is important that all staff members at least understand Tech Prep. Ideally, you want as many staff members as possible to be involved. The more involvement you have at the building level, the more effective the program will be.

Use the worksheet (page 52) and the sample memorandum of invitation (page 50) to help create the building team.

Building Team Worksheet

1. Identify the people who will serve on the Building Teams.

_____

Building Name

Name	Position	Phone
_____	_____	_____
_____	_____	_____
_____	_____	_____
_____	_____	_____
_____	_____	_____
_____	_____	_____

_____

Building Name

Name	Position	Phone
_____	_____	_____
_____	_____	_____
_____	_____	_____
_____	_____	_____
_____	_____	_____
_____	_____	_____

Organizing the Postsecondary School

We recommend creating two kinds of teams at the postsecondary level. The first kind of team focuses attention on articulation agreements, and the second focuses on curriculum integration and application.

The articulation teams at the postsecondary school are responsible for building a nonduplicative course of study within the career programs. Each career program will need an articulation team. Responsibilities of the articulation team are identified below.

1. Compile current competency lists for coursework offered in the career program.
2. Share competencies with secondary teachers who teach related courses.
3. Create a course sequence within the program from secondary to postsecondary that eliminates duplication of coursework.
4. Develop a signed agreement that identifies the nonduplicative sequence of courses and recommended electives.

Each articulation team should be composed of a program director and several faculty members. We recommend that a team chairperson be appointed to oversee and coordinate the activities of the team. The process of creating an articulation agreement will take at least two meetings.

Articulation Team Worksheet

_____

Name of Career Program

Members of Articulation Team:

_____

_____

_____

_____

_____

_____

Goals of the Articulation Team:

_____

_____

_____

_____

_____

_____

Curriculum Integration Teams

Curriculum integration teams are responsible for promoting changes in teaching strategies at the college or university. These teams should be composed of faculty from a variety of career programs and academic disciplines. There should be a chairperson responsible for facilitating the meetings. The responsibilities of each team may vary greatly. Below are two possible responsibilities for these teams. It is important for these teams to develop projects that are most suited to the students within the local programs.

Develop Opportunities for Integrating Curriculum Across Disciplines. This may include team teaching strategies between and among English, communication, history, psychology, sociology, economics, and other disciplines.

Create Opportunities for Integrating Career Development into Classrooms. This activity may include faculty from career programs as well as other disciplines. Many faculty members are not aware of how their disciplines are used within various careers and employment opportunities. Faculty who teach within career programs often can provide the application that allows students to see the usefulness of what they are learning.

Curriculum Integration Team Worksheet

Members of Curriculum Integration Team:

_____

_____

_____

_____

_____

_____

Goals of the Team:

_____

_____

_____

_____

_____

_____

_____

6

Conducting In-Services

M any people will be involved in the development of the Tech Prep program. We suggest you first provide in-service programs for participants so that a common understanding can be created.

Who Needs In-Service Programs?

Anyone who will play a key role in the development of the program should be trained first. Additional participants will also need in-service training; however, we recommend focusing first on the members of the steering committee, the work team members, the action and building team members, and the articulation and curriculum integration teams. After these people have received an orientation, you should turn your attention to additional groups.

First, provide orientation to the steering committee, consortium work teams, school district teams, and postsecondary teams. Once the key players have received an orientation to Tech Prep, you should turn your attention to such groups as faculty and staff at all consortium schools, community members, school boards, and business and industry personnel.

In-Service Topics

There are two specific topics we believe all key players must understand before they can be effective members of the project. These components are:

1. The meaning of a Tech Prep Program.
2. The role each of them is being asked to play.

Understanding the Tech Prep Program

It is important that the work team members have a solid understanding of the program and its specific goals. We suggest providing in-service programs and/or workshops on several topics to help the members of work teams understand the project.

To provide a complete understanding of Tech Prep, we suggest including all the following topics within the first in-service program:

- What is a Tech Prep program?
- Why is a Tech Prep program needed?
- What is a Tech Prep consortium?
- What kinds of changes will a Tech Prep program require?

Understanding One's Role in the Tech Prep Program

The key players must also understand their own roles in the Tech Prep Program. All work team members must understand what is expected of them. This includes knowing:

- How often they will be meeting
- How much time will be needed for meetings and for work outside meetings
- How long the team will exist
- What the team's specific responsibilities will be

After an in-service program has been provided for the key players, attention can be turned to additional groups. Some groups can be addressed by the consortium staff; however, it will not be possible for the consortium staff to provide all in-service training. Each consortium member must identify specific local audiences that should be informed and make arrangements to provide the appropriate in-service training. We make the following suggestions for local in-service programs:

District Level

- The Board of Education should receive a full explanation and regular updates of the program and changes being made for the Tech Prep program
- Advisory groups that work with the school system will need to know about Tech Prep and the changes being made

High School Level

- Local parent groups should be informed about Tech Prep and the changes it will bring to the school
- All faculty and staff should be aware of Tech Prep and the changes it will bring

Postsecondary Level

- The Board of Education must be aware of Tech Prep and the changes it will bring to the college
- As many faculty and staff at the college as possible should be informed about Tech Prep and how it will affect students coming into the college
- Advisory councils should be aware of and involved in Tech Prep

Basic Presentations

We suggest creating three different basic presentations on Tech Prep. These can be used on different occasions as necessary. The presentation you use will depend on the audience you are addressing.

Model 1

This is a 15-minute presentation designed to familiarize your audience with the basics of Tech Prep. Typically, this presentation will contain one or two transparencies from the changing work-place section, one or two (if any) from the education section, and two or three from the Tech Prep definition section. You may use this presentation for community and other related audiences. This is a short presentation that contains the bare minimum.

Model 2

This is a 30- or 45-minute presentation designed for audiences who need to know more than the basics of Tech Prep. You should add transparencies from the section that is most appropriate for your audience. For example, boards of education may need more information from the transparencies on the Tech Prep definition section than from the education section. This presentation should contain more specific information for an audience that is more highly motivated.

Model 3

This is a presentation of an hour or longer designed for audiences who are directly related to the Tech Prep project. Typically, this presentation is given to teachers, counselors, and other education professionals. Transparencies used should reflect each of the sections equally (workplace, education, and Tech Prep).

Transparency Masters

We have provided some transparency masters for your convenience. They are designed to address three main topics:

The Changing Workforce
Our future depends upon a highly skilled workforce
Technology has increased the skill levels required for workers
Agriculture (plow to biotechnology)
Manufacturing (assembly line to robotics)
Information (typewriters to voice to print)
Employment shift from manufacturing to service
Trends of the future (a)
Trends of the future (b)

Education Issues
The problem
Education (K-16) must change
75% of high school graduates do not receive a 4 year degree
What happens to high school graduates?
The new basic skills
SCANS three-part foundation
SCANS Competencies

Tech Prep
What is Tech Prep?
Who is Tech Prep for?
Components of Tech Prep
Functions of a Consortium

Course sequence
Course sequences built around career clusters
Three levels of proficiency

We recommend that you add transparencies that relate to your local project.

Transparency Masters

The Changing Workforce

Our future depends upon a highly skilled workforce

Technology has increased the skill levels required for workers

Agriculture has moved from the plow and the mule to genetically altering foods using biotechnology

Manufacturing has moved from assembly line workers to robots and technicians who maintain them

Information processing has moved from manual typewriters and keypunch to voice-to-print technology and Personal Data Assistants (PDA)

Employment has shifted from manufacturing to service.

Trends of the Future

60% of high school students will work in jobs that currently do not exist

90% of all jobs in the year 2000 will require knowledge of a computer

85% of future jobs will require skill training beyond high school

80% of future jobs will require some college but less than a 4 year degree

Trends of the Future

The average adult changes jobs 7 times and changes careers 3 times over his or her work life

The new workforce will work predominantly in small companies (25 employees or less)

The workforce will be predominantly female, older, and multicultural

Education Issues

The Problem!

- Our education system was not designed to produce highly skilled workers.

- The system was designed for an economy based on unskilled labor.

Education (K-16) Must Change

- ■ Since 1989, one-third of the jobs requiring a bachelor's degree have disappeared.

- ■ By 2005, only 30% of jobs will require a bachelor's degree.

- ■ 75% of the new jobs created in the next ten years will require some college but less than a four-year degree.

75% of high school graduates do not receive a 4 year degree

yet

Our curriculum is designed for students bound for a 4 year college degree

What Happens to High School Graduates?

1980 55% Entered college

45% Did not enter college

1982 31% Still enrolled in college

67% Not enrolled

1987 24% Bachelor's degree

8% Arts and sciences

2% Graduate

3% Professional

16% Professional fields

The New Basic Skills

- ■ Learning to learn
- ■ Reading, Writing, Computation
- ■ Listening and Oral Communication
- ■ Creative Thinking/Problem Solving

SOURCE: From *Workplace Basics: The Skills Employers Want*, Carnevale, Gainer, and Meltzer, © copyright 1988 by U.S. Department of Labor, Employment and Training Administration.

SCANS*

Three-Part Foundation

■ **Basic Skills**

■ **Thinking Skills**

■ **Personal Qualities**

*Secretary's Commission on Achieving Necessary Skills

Five SCANS* Competencies

- **Resources**
- **Interpersonal**
- **Information**
- **Systems**
- **Technology**

*Secretary's Commission on Achieving Necessary Skills

Tech Prep

What Is Tech Prep?

A technical education program that begins in high school and culminates with an associate degree or 2 year certificate

Who Is Tech Prep For?

Job Training → Employment

General Education → ???????

College Preparation → 4 Year Degree

Components of Tech Prep

1. Course sequences

2. Sequences built around career clusters

3. Three proficiency levels

4. Application-based teaching strategies

5. Integration of disciplines and subjects

6. Involvement of business and industry

Functions of a Consortium

1. Provide linkages among members

2. Provide in-service programs to consortium members

3. Identify tomorrow's career opportunities

4. Structure the career clusters

5. Assist schools with promotion

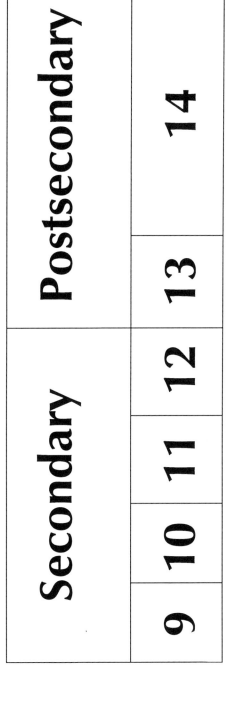

Course Sequence

Secondary			Postsecondary	
9	10	11	12	13	14

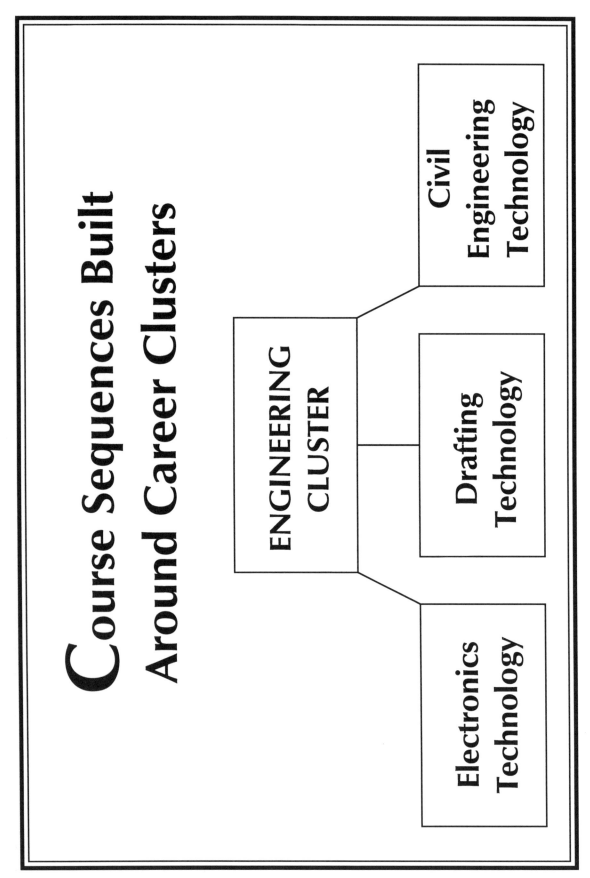

Course Sequences Built Around Career Clusters

ENGINEERING CLUSTER

Electronics Technology

Drafting Technology

Civil Engineering Technology

Three Levels of Proficiency

Specialty Proficiencies
(Postsecondary)

Technical Proficiencies
(High School and Technical School)

Core Proficiencies
(High School)

7

Modifying the Curriculum

The Sequence of Courses

A Tech Prep program presents a sequence of courses beginning in high school and culminating with an associate degree or 2 year certificate. This sequence of courses should do the following:

1. Replace the "general education" sequence of courses in high school.
2. Include courses that cover the core, technical, and specialty proficiencies.
3. Run parallel to the traditional "college bound" sequence of courses in high school.
4. Raise expectations for student performance.
5. Be an option for all students.
6. Provide advanced skills for program graduates.

There are three levels of proficiency within a Tech Prep program. The next section discusses the three proficiency levels.

Level 1: Core proficiencies (high school) of math, science, communication, and technology
Level 2: Technical proficiencies (high school and technical school)
Level 3: Specialty proficiencies (postsecondary)

Level 1: The Core Proficiencies

Core proficiencies are the required skills in mathematics, science, communication, and technology for all Tech Prep students. The curriculum work team should identify the core proficiencies for the Tech Prep program. These proficiencies help schools to create a common set of basic requirements for Tech Prep students. Whenever many secondary schools are feeding students into the same postsecondary school, it is essential to have training to skills at approximately the same level. Assuming that the secondary school consortium members will make their own curriculum changes, it is essential to have those curriculum changes grounded in a set of core proficiencies. All schools address the core proficiencies; however, each one may do so in a different way.

The core proficiencies can be established by the curriculum work team or an ad hoc group created by the curriculum work team. Each consortium should establish the content areas that the core will touch. The set of core proficiencies for our consortium are contained in Appendix C.

Level 2: Technical Proficiencies

Technical proficiencies are the introductory skills within a career cluster or program. They are also the technical skills necessary for entrance into and effective performance in the postsecondary career program.

Level 3: Specialty Proficiencies

Specialty proficiencies are the skills required for successful employment within a specific occupation. The third level of proficiencies addressed by a Tech Prep program, these are taught at the postsecondary institution. Typically, these sequences of courses already are in place.

Articulation is the process of aligning the secondary and postsecondary curricula so that there is a sequenced, nonduplicated program of study. This may include awarding students advanced standing credit at the postsecondary school for the proficiencies they already can demonstrate. After a Tech Prep program is up and running, and when students entering the postsecondary degree programs are demonstrating the appropriate skills, the sequence of courses that encompasses the specialty proficiencies can be elevated. This will allow students to graduate from the degree program with a higher level of skills.

	9	10	11	12	13	14
ENGLISH						
MATH						
SCIENCE						
HUMANITIES/ SOCIAL SCIENCE						
OTHER REQUIREMENTS						
TECHNOLOGY						
TECHNOLOGY						

Chart 7.1.

Creating the Sequence of Courses

Begin with a grid that identifies the year in school and the content areas covered. This form can be used to "plug in" the courses within the sequence. Chart 7.1 is a sample blank form.

STEP 1: Identify specific courses required for high school graduation. Place these courses on the grid.

STEP 2: Identify the courses that will address the core proficiencies designed by the curriculum work team. Place these on the grid in the appropriate squares.

STEP 3: Postsecondary faculty (with advice from business and industry representatives) identify the technical proficiencies. These are typically the skills needed by students entering the postsecondary degree program.

STEP 4: Secondary and postsecondary faculty identify the courses that address the technical proficiencies. These can be taught at the high school or vocational-technical center.

BLUE VALLEY SCHOOLS TECH PREP SEQUENCE

9	10	11	12
ENGLISH I	ENGLISH II	ENGLISH III	CONTEMPORARY COMMUNICATION
MATH I OR ALGEBRA I	MATH II / GEOMETRY	MATH III / ADVANCED ALGEBRA	ALGEBRA II OR PRE CALC OR ALGEBRA III
BIOLOGICAL & PHYSICAL SCIENCE REQUIREMENTS		SCIENCE & TECHNOLOGY I SYSTEMS	ADVANCED TECHNOLOGY II SYSTEMS
PHYSICAL EDUCATION	WORLD HISTORY	AMERICAN HISTORY	AMERICAN GOVERNMENT (1/2) / SOCIAL STUDIES ELECTIVE (1/2)
KEYBOARDING (1/2) / COMPUTER REQUIREMENT	HEALTH (1/2) / ELECTIVE (1/2)	TECH PREP ELECTIVES	

ENGINEERING & INDUSTRIAL TECHNOLOGY CLUSTER

This sequence of courses prepares students to enter the degree programs listed below:

Associate of Applied Science Degree
  Automotive Technology
  Heating, Ventilation & Air Conditioning Technology

Associate of Science Degree
  Civil Engineering Technology
  Drafting Technology
  Electronics Engineering Technology

TECH PREP ELECTIVES*

Drafting I	Automotive Technology (JCTEC)
Drafting II	Career Exploration
Drafting III	Advanced Industrial Technology
Industrial Technology I	

*Students must take at least 2 Tech Prep Electives
Tech Prep Electives may provide advanced standing credit at JCCC

Chart 7.2.

STEP 5: Secondary and postsecondary faculty sequence the courses so that students can move easily from high school into the postsecondary degree program.

STEP 6: Place these courses in the appropriate squares on the grid.

STEP 7: Postsecondary faculty (with advice from business and industry representatives) identify the specialty proficiencies for completion of the program.

STEP 8: Place these courses in the appropriate squares on the grid.

Samples for Review

Chart 7.2 contains a sample Tech Prep sequence for an engineering and industrial technology cluster. The sequence covers only the core and technical proficiencies.

Chart 7.3 contains a sample articulation agreement for Tech Prep. The agreement lays out the last 2 years of high school and 2

Tech Prep Associate Degree Consortium of Johnson/Douglas Counties
Articulation Agreement
between
Blue Valley Schools and Johnson County Community College
in the
Engineering & Industrial Technology Cluster
Drafting Technology Program
Civil Option

Grade 11	Grade 12	Grade 13	Grade 14
English III	Contemporary Communication	Technical Drafting	Civil Drafting
		Intro to CAD Concepts	CAD 3-D Technical Elective
Math III or Algebra II	Algebra II or Pre Calc or Algebra III	Intro to Personal Computers	
		PC DOS	Technical Statics & Mechanics
Science & Technology I or Chemistry I	Science & Technology II or Physics	Composition I	Technical Physics I
		Technical Math I	Electrical Drafting
		CPCA Elective	Structural Drafting
American History	American Government (1/2) Social Studies Elective (1/2)	Interpreting Arch Drawings	Technical Elective
		Intermediate CAD	Social Science & or Economics Elective
Drafting II*		Construction Methods	
	Drafting III*	Technical Writing I	Humanities & or Art Elective
Elective			
	Elective	Technical Math II	Health & or Physical Education Elective

Tech Prep Electives	Technical Electives	
Industrial Technology	Intro to Word Processing	Windows
Career Exploration	Spreadsheets on Micro I	Civil Drafting
Introduction to Computer Programming BASIC*	Database on Micro I	CAD Applications
Advanced Computer Programming BASIC*	Drafting Internship I	Drafting Intern II
	Intro Electronics	Intro to Welding
	Machine Tool Processes	Metallurgy
	Any one of the following programming classes	
	Programming Algorithms	
	Basic for Engineering Technology	
	Programming Fundamentals	
	Programming for Engineering & Science	
*Provides advanced standing credit at JCCC.		

Chart 7.3.

TECH PREP ADVANCED STANDING AGREEMENT

between

Blue Valley Public Schools and Johnson County Community College

in the

Business & Information Technology Cluster

Data Processing

The courses listed below have been reviewed by the program director and faculty at Johnson County Community College. These courses have been found to be equivalent in content and are acceptable for Advanced Standing Credit - Tech Prep. The awarding of advanced standing credit for Tech Prep is subject to the Tech Prep Advanced Standing Policies listed below.

1) Advanced standing credit -Tech Prep applies only to students officially enrolled in the Tech Prep Associate Degree Consortium of Johnson/Douglas Counties.
2) Credit will be applied only for courses identified on a Tech Prep advanced standing agreement form.
3) Credit will be posted on the JCCC transcript as Advanced Standing Credit - Tech Prep.
4) The JCCC equivalent course will be posted on the transcript.
5) Advanced Standing Credit - Tech Prep will be given only for a final grade of "C" or better.
6) The grade will be posted as "P".
7) Credit will be posted after 12 additional hours of JCCC credit have been successfully completed.
8) No fee will be assessed for the credit.
9) Credits may not apply toward the JCCC residency requirement.
10) A maximum of 12 credit hours will be accepted by JCCC for Advanced Standing Credit - Tech Prep.

Secondary Courses*:   **Johnson County Community College Courses:**

Course Number/Name	Credit Hours	Course Number/Name		Credit Hours
Drafting II	1	DRAF 120	Basic Drafting	2
Drafting III	1	DRAF 130	Intro to CAD Concepts	3

_____   _____

Secondary Administrator   Date   Dean of Instruction   Date

* Course outlines for each course must be attached.

Chart 7.4.

years of college (4 year map). It also identifies any overlapping curriculum for which advanced standing credit may be granted.

Chart 7.4 contains a sample Tech Prep Advanced Standing Credit form that can be used to formalize an agreement on overlapping curriculum.

Applied/Integrated Teaching Strategies

Traditionally, subjects are taught as though they do not overlap. Applied/integrated teaching strategies allow subjects and disciplines to be blended together. Students begin to understand how subjects are related and why the content is useful. The courses included in your sequence for Tech Prep students must be taught using applied/integrated teaching strategies.

Applied/integrated teaching strategies shift the focus of the classroom from theory to application, use "hands-on" approaches to learning, answer the question, "Why do I need this?," build connections between academic and technical learning, and build connections among subject areas (e.g., biology and chemistry, physics and math, or music and math).

There are any number of ways to apply and integrate teaching. The following section presents some suggestions for using application and integration teaching strategies. It is crucial that these suggestions be used as a starting place and that you also look beyond these suggestions.

Team Teaching

Team teaching can connect teachers and expand their skills while creating an exciting learning environment for students. The following pairs should be considered for team teaching.

Academic and Technical

This team can be a very effective approach to applying teaching strategies. The academic teacher can provide content-specific knowledge while the technical teacher provides the application for the content.

Academic and Academic

This team is most effective when two disciplines are integrated. Science and math, for example, complement each other well in the classroom. The math teacher, for example, can explain the formulas and manipulations within the science experiment.

Technical and Technical

The pairing of technical teachers also works well. For example, a computer-assisted design (CAD) system can help interior design students with room layout. Most home economics teachers, however, do not have the skills to run the CAD system. Drafting students will also learn a lot about working with clients if they treat the interior design students as such.

Applied Academics Curriculum

Another way to teach using application and integration is to use an "applied academic" curriculum. This is a curriculum that has been developed through a consortium process and is available for sale. "Applied academic" curricula can offer teachers direction for modifying their teaching. We recommend using caution whenever a prepackaged curriculum is purchased. Teachers must modify the curriculum to fit the needs of their students.

Principles of Technology

This is an applied physics curriculum produced by the Center for Occupational Research and Development (CORD). It is designed for high school students and usually is taught in the junior and senior years.

Applied Mathematics

This is a hands-on mathematics curriculum (produced by CORD) that teaches approximately the equivalent of algebra I and geometry. It was designed with occupational application "labs" that help students see how mathematics concepts are used in various jobs.

Applied Biology/Chemistry

This is a hands-on curriculum designed by CORD for high school students. It combines the subjects of biology and chemistry using "real-life" applications of the concepts.

Applied Communication

This is a hands-on curriculum designed by the Agency for Instructional Technology (AIT). It focuses on teaching communication skills and can be taught as an independent course or used one module at a time.

Workplace Readiness

This is a three-unit curriculum designed by AIT. The curriculum can be used within a classroom or learning lab.

Applied Economics

There are several different applied economics curriculum packages available. Typically, this is a high school curriculum that teaches practical application of economics concepts.

The Hierarchy of Integration

The National Center for Research in Vocational Education (NCRVE) has conducted several descriptive research studies on the integration of academic and vocational education. It has identified a five-step hierarchy of integration. From simple to complex, the hierarchy includes basic infusion, advanced infusion, applied academics, curriculum alignment, and restructured schools.

Here is a description of the five levels in the hierarchy.

BASIC INFUSION
> Attempting to improve the academic skills of students by incorporating academic content into vocational courses

ADVANCED INFUSION
> Vocational and academic teachers work together to integrate academic skills into vocational classes

APPLIED ACADEMICS
> Curricula for academic education are modified to incorporate vocational applications

CURRICULUM ALIGNMENT
> Vocational and academic classes reinforce one another, both laterally and sequentially

RESTRUCTURED SCHOOLS
> A curriculum (formed) around an occupational specialty, depending on close alliances with the business community

In addition to teaching strategies and systemic reform models of integration, the following activities are suggested as facilitating the integration process.

- Team building
- Linking professional development activities with the establishment of a teacher team

- Allowing teachers to teach teachers
- Delegating responsibility for integration through specific assignments
- Scheduling creatively to allow time when teachers could benefit by sharing information
- Empowering teachers by allowing them to become "owners" of the integration process

Beginning Curriculum Changes

Some of the curriculum changes require action by the school district as a whole, whereas other changes must be initiated and carried out at each high school. We make the following recommendations of tasks to initiate curriculum changes within the school district.

District Level

1. The action team should develop the sequence of courses that covers the core competencies.
2. Appropriate representatives from the technical areas (such as business and drafting) should work with the postsecondary representatives to establish the courses that cover the technical proficiencies.

High School Level

1. Each high school should begin to modify its curriculum in every discipline. Teachers should begin to use integrated/applied learning strategies, lower-level courses should be dropped from the curriculum, and alternative delivery modes should be investigated, such as team teaching and block scheduling.
2. High school counselors must become familiar with the curriculum changes being made so they can place appropriate students in the classes.

Postsecondary Level

1. Career program faculty should identify entrance requirements for their program.
2. Identify advanced skills to be taught when the articulation agreements are in place.

Reference

Schmidt, B. June, Finch, Curtis R., & Faulkner, Susan. (1992). *Integrating vocational and academic education: A practitioner's guide.* Berkeley, CA: National Center for Research in Vocational Education.

8

Involving People From Local Businesses

Involving business and industry in the Tech Prep program is one of the keys to success. Remember that one of the goals of a Tech Prep program is to bridge the gap between the classroom and the workplace. There are many ways to involve business and industry personnel in the Tech Prep program. Typical activities and forms of involvement are discussed below.

Activities to Involve Business and Industry

1. Representatives on the steering committee
2. Representatives on work teams
3. Validation of proficiencies
4. Speakers within the classroom
5. Curriculum writing
6. Classroom/work exchange
7. Shadowing/mentorships/internships
8. Apprenticeships

1. Representatives on the Steering Committee

Most Tech Prep programs have representatives from business and industry serving on the steering committee. Not only is their expertise helpful in designing the program, but their involvement helps them to "buy in" early in the project.

2. Representatives on Work Teams

As the consortium steering committee creates various work teams to design and implement the program, you will find expertise available in business and industry representatives. Including these individuals on the work teams provides you with expertise and provides involvement from the business representative.

3. Validation of Proficiencies

It is important to know that the proficiencies addressed in the program represent current workplace skills. Representatives from various fields can help validate the proficiencies within the program. When asking for validation of proficiencies, be sure to ask a worker who is currently employed in that position. Sometimes managers are removed from the everyday activities of employees.

4. Speakers Within the Classroom

Most business and industry personnel are happy to talk with students about a given topic. We suggest providing specific information about what you would like the speaker to address, time available, and who the audience will be. Most people are only too happy to help.

5. Curriculum Writing

Business and industry personnel are very familiar with workplace skills. Tasks that are everyday business activities can make excellent learning experiences for students. For example, dealing with a full "in basket" is a typical business task. Students can learn a great deal about decision making by attempting to handle their own "in basket." Getting employees involved in writing curriculum is an excellent way to modify the classroom. This can be done through the consortium or through an individual school.

6. Classroom/Work Exchange

Suppose that teachers could exchange places with employees of a local business. The exchange program should be well defined in advance, outlining such details as length of exchange and duties of each person on the "new" job. Imagine the walls that would drop after spending a day in a totally new job!

Business representatives are used to serving on teams that are "active," rather than teams that discuss and debate. Be sure that your teams are action oriented. This will help you maintain the involvement of business and industry representatives.

7. Shadowing/Mentorships/Internships

When people think of shadowing, mentorships, and internships, they typically think of students. It would be just as powerful for teachers and staff to participate in these kinds of programs. Before teachers will recommend an activity to students, they must believe it is worthwhile.

8. Apprenticeships

Business and industry personnel are essential to developing effective apprenticeship programs. It is difficult for some educators to "let go of the power" in this type of education experience. Many trade areas have specific apprenticeship requirements. You should consult local trade unions for additional information.

Whose Responsibility Is It?

Educators often want to know whose responsibility it is to get business and industry involved in the Tech Prep program. Some tasks can be handled by the consortium coordinator, but some must be taken on by the local district.

Business and industry representatives who serve on the steering committee or work teams typically are appointed by the consortium. The consortium also can handle validating the proficiencies. Other activities, such as arranging speakers within the classroom, curriculum writing, classroom/work exchange, and shadowing/mentorships/internships, can be initiated by a local school. The Tech Prep action or building team probably should take responsibility for initiating these kinds of activities.

The business and industry survey (Figure 8.1) can be used—after a presentation has been given to a chamber of commerce, Optimist club, or other business organization—to obtain names of people who are willing to help your Tech Prep efforts.

BUSINESS & INDUSTRY SURVEY

The Tech Prep project is building technical education programs which begin in high school and culminate with a two year associate degree or certificate. The program includes a sequence of courses which are grounded in workplace application. In order to build an effective program we need your input. Would you, or someone in your organization, be willing to help us bring education and the workplace closer together?

Please check any of the areas below in which your organization would be willing to help us. THANKS!

___ Establish work competencies for a program. Check the particular area below:
    ___ General workplace skills   ___ Business Technologies
    ___ Merchandising   ___ Engineering Technologies
    ___ Industrial Technologies   ___ Health Technologies
    ___ Human Services   ___ Other _____

___ Validate work competencies
___ Provide an internship for a teacher
___ Provide an internship for a student
___ Allow students and educators to visit your workplace
___ Work with a school to help the teachers implement workplace applications in the classroom
___ Serve as a guest speaker
___ Serve as an advisor to a local school

___ I am unable to help you right now, however, I would like to be kept informed about the project.

Please let us know how we can reach you.

_____
Name   Organization

_____
Mailing Address   Phone

Figure 8.1. Business and Industry Involvement Survey

9

Promoting Your Program

The program must be promoted by the consortium and the local schools. Each member of the consortium should promote the Tech Prep program in the home district. The promotion work team should coordinate consortium efforts to promote the Tech Prep program. The action and building teams should also work on promoting the program within the districts.

Steps in Building a Campaign

The steps in designing a promotion "campaign" are relatively simple, although the process of actually designing the campaign usually is not so simple. The steps identified below should help focus promotion efforts whether they are performed by the consortium or by a local school.

What Audience Do You Want to Reach?

The first step in any promotion campaign is to identify your audience. Usually, there are several groups of people you will want to reach. Identifying as many of these groups as you can will make the message easier to design.

Typical audiences for Tech Prep promotion campaigns include teachers, students, parents, business and industry personnel, local community members, school board members, and chamber of commerce executive board members.

What Do You Want the Audience to Do or Believe?

Ultimately, the goal of a promotion campaign is to get some action or change in belief from your audience. When identifying the outcome(s) you want from your audiences, be as specific as you can. Remember that it is possible to have more than one outcome for a single audience.

Typical outcomes of a Tech Prep promotion campaign may include the following:

> **Teachers:** Adapt teaching strategies to include application and integration.
> **Students:** Enroll in the Tech Prep program.
> **School Board:** Actively promote the Tech Prep program within the district.

What Does the Audience Already Know or Believe?

Finding out what your audience already knows about a Tech Prep program and related issues is helpful in designing the campaign. You need to know at least whether to expect a hostile or supportive reception! Below are three common methods of gaining this information:

- Survey (written, phone)
- Informal networking (talking with community representatives)
- Local environmental scan (newspaper, radio, editorials)

The method you use to identify what the audience already knows should fit your local situation. For example, some small school districts are keenly aware of their parents', students', and local community's perceptions. Consequently, a less formal data collection process is necessary.

How Can You Reach the Audience?

It is important to identify methods that can be used to reach your audiences. You may be able to reach more than one audience with the same method. Typical methods used to reach Tech Prep audiences include:

- Public presentations
- Written communication (brochures, newsletters)
- Newspaper articles
- Special events
- Radio announcements

Once you have identified the audience, outcome, perceptions and methods, you can begin to design the activities to accomplish your goal.

For example:

AUDIENCE: Students

DESIRED OUTCOME: Enroll in Tech Prep

PERCEPTIONS: Unaware of Tech Prep, unaware of employment options

METHODS: Video, student newspaper, announcements, posters, counselor conferences, teacher encouragement, Tech Prep activities

The promotion work team should decide which activities it will perform and which activities might be performed by the local schools. Some promotion efforts should be performed by the consortium, whereas others must be accomplished by each school district. A video, for example, usually is a consortium product, whereas an advertisement in the school newspaper might be local to each high school.

The final piece of the promotion campaign is to design and "send" the message itself. Identify which of the methods you wish to use in the campaign. This may be done by the consortium promotion work team or by the action/building teams. For each message to be designed, you should answer the questions below:

1. What steps must be taken to create this message?
2. Who will be responsible for the activity?
3. What is the time frame to complete this activity?

Example: Audience = Students   Method = Video

What steps must be taken to create this message?
1. Obtain/create the video
2. Identify which students will see the video
3. Identify when students will see the video
4. Plan feedback/discussion

Who will be responsible for this activity?

1. Media coordinator will secure the video
2. Assistant principal will coordinate identification of students and set the schedule for viewing the video
3. Teachers will run the feedback session

What is the time frame for this activity?

1. Video selected by November
2. Identification of students and viewing schedule completed by December
3. Viewing and feedback sessions during February

Promotion Worksheet

Take a moment to complete this worksheet to organize your promotion campaign.

1. Identify the audience you want to reach.

_____

_____

_____

_____

2. What action or belief do you want from this audience?

_____

_____

_____

_____

3. Describe what the audience already knows or believes about Tech Prep.

_____

_____

_____

_____

Promotion Worksheet, Continued

4. How can you reach this audience?

_____

_____

_____

_____

What steps must be taken to create this message?

_____

_____

_____

_____

Who will be responsible for this activity?

_____

_____

_____

_____

What is the time frame for this activity?

_____

_____

_____

_____

10

Tracking Your Success

Evaluation is an important piece of any reform process. Although we are not evaluation experts, we do want to introduce some of the issues you will deal with as you evaluate Tech Prep. We strongly advise consulting with evaluation experts in designing an evaluation plan.

Answering Key Questions About Evaluating Tech Prep

It is just now possible to draw conclusions about the effectiveness of Tech Prep programs that began many years ago. It is important to generate some baseline data on your students and programs so that you will have a comparison point.

There are several key questions to be answered in designing an evaluation plan for Tech Prep. These questions should be used by the evaluation work team.

How Will the Data Be Used?

We suggest that you discuss what will be done with the results of your evaluation. Is the evaluation being conducted for federal, state, or local administrative reporting, and/or local promotion of the program? Knowing how the data will be used will help ensure that you collect the appropriate data.

What Data Elements Will Be Collected?

Generally, you will want to collect some demographic data about the students in the program. These data help you describe your population and make comparisons to other populations. You may also want to collect academic performance indicators on students (e.g., test scores, grades). These can be used to show increased student performance. Consider the availability of pre- and posttest scores. Another kind of data you may want to collect is descriptive data from students, for example, a measure of how they feel about the program.

Where Are the Data Available?

Consider where you will be able to obtain the data you want to collect. Some information will be housed in the school district office or the high school itself. Still other information may need to be collected from students in a survey format.

How Will the Data Be Maintained?

Consider what resources are available for maintaining the data. Can they be kept on a computer system, or will they be on paper? The answer to this question may determine how much data you collect and the kinds of reports you can generate.

How Can Immediate Gains Be Measured?

Schools can begin to measure changes by monitoring some local elements. We suggest that each high school keep track of the following kinds of information as the changes come on line.

1. Enrollments in courses affected by curriculum changes.
2. Number of students enrolled in science and math courses.
3. Sections of study hall offered.
4. Student grades.
5. Scores on standard tests taken by students.
6. Students' and teachers' perceptions of the changes.
7. Parents' perceptions of the changes.

All this information can be reported to local audiences such as the board of education, parents, and community groups.

Evaluation Worksheet

1. Identify how the data you collect will be used.

_____

_____

_____

_____

2. List the data elements you will collect and identify the source for each element.

    DATA ELEMENT   SOURCE

_____

_____

_____

_____

_____

_____

_____

_____

3. Describe how the data will be maintained.

_____

_____

_____

Resource A: Definitions

Action team: A team created within a school district to handle decisions and activities that affect the school district as a whole.

AIT: The Agency for Instructional Technology, which produces curriculum packages (e.g., Applied Communication and Workplace Readiness).

Application teaching strategies: Those teaching strategies that promote the learning of practical applications. These teaching strategies respond to the question, "When will I ever use this?"

Applied academics: A prepackaged curriculum that teaches traditional academic subjects in a hands-on fashion.

Articulation agreement (Tech Prep): An agreement that lays out a sequence of courses bridging the high school and the postsecondary institution. Articulation agreements typically focus on career programs.

Articulation team: A group of faculty (secondary and postsecondary) who are responsible for developing articulation agreements.

Building team: A group of high school teachers and staff members responsible for implementing Tech Prep within a high school.

Business and industry involvement work team: A work team created by the Tech Prep steering committee that is responsible for getting business and industry representatives involved in the Tech Prep project.

Career cluster: A group of related occupations in which there are 2 year degree or certificate programs available.

Consortium (Tech Prep): A group of schools that work together to develop a Tech Prep program. It must have a minimum of one secondary and one postsecondary school.

CORD: The Center for Occupational Research and Development. It produces applied curriculum packages (e.g., Applied Mathematics, Applied Biology/Chemistry, and Principles of Technology).

Core proficiencies: The required skills in mathematics, science, communication, and technology required of all Tech Prep students.

Curriculum work team: A team created by the Tech Prep steering committee to oversee curriculum changes that affect all consortium schools.

Evaluation work team: A team created by the Tech Prep steering committee to build and implement an evaluation plan.

Integration teaching strategies: Those teaching strategies that build connections among subjects and disciplines (e.g., biology and chemistry, history and mathematics).

NCRVE: National Center for Research in Vocational Education.

Neglected majority: The group of students who are not enrolled in a traditional college preparatory or vocational preparatory sequence.

Postsecondary school: A community college or technical school.

Promotion work team: A team created by the Tech Prep steering committee to design and implement a promotion campaign for Tech Prep.

SCANS: Secretary's Commission on Achieving Necessary Skills.

Secondary school: A high school, typically housing Grades 9-12 or 10-12.

Sequence of courses: A nonduplicative progression of courses recommended for Tech Prep students. A sequence includes academic and technical courses on the secondary and postsecondary levels.

Specialty proficiencies: The skills required for successful employment in a specific occupation.

Steering committee (Tech Prep): The main committee responsible for the implementation of a Tech Prep program. Members typically include at least one representative from each member of the consortium and business and industry representatives.

Tech Prep: A technical education program beginning in high school and culminating with an associate degree or 2 year certificate.

Technical proficiencies: The introductory skills within a career cluster or program.

Resource B:
Core Proficiencies

The following proficiencies were identified by the Tech Prep Associate Degree Consortium of Johnson/Douglas Counties.

Core Proficiencies

Science

1. Demonstrate the science process skills.

   The student should be able to correctly observe, analyze data, conduct an experiment, etc.

2. Demonstrate an acceptable level of specific content.

   The student should be able to demonstrate knowledge of systems, biological processes, physical principles, etc.

3. Apply the science process skills to investigating problems.

   The student should design and/or perform laboratory experiments to investigate various phenomena.

4. Recognize the interrelationships of science, technology, health, and the environment.

   Interrelationships should provide the student with an understanding of how technology, environmental, and health industries draw on scientific principles to resolve problems. Courses should incorporate computer usage.

5. Work independently, collaboratively, and safely.

Courses should include exercises that allow both independent and collaborative experiences. Safety concepts and principles should be incorporated throughout the courses.

Mathematics

All Tech Prep students should have, as a minimum, preparation for college algebra before entering the postsecondary portion of the Tech Prep program.

1. Apply mathematical problem-solving strategies to problems both within and outside mathematics.

Understand algebraic concepts, geometry concepts, functions, probability and statistics, and discrete mathematics.

2. Recognize mathematics as an integrated whole.

Make connections among mathematical topics, between mathematics and other disciplines, and between mathematics and real-world applications.

3. Communicate mathematically using the language and symbols of mathematics.

Understand estimation, formal proofs, and inductive/deductive reasoning.

Technology

1. Understand the role of technology in today's marketplace.

Understand the impact of technology advancement on business, industry, and the job market. Technologies might include artificial intelligence and biogenetics.

2. Demonstrate computer literacy skills.

Understand the components of computers, demonstrate software application skills, and understand basic file management techniques for computers.

3. Comprehend the impact of technology on various social systems.

Understand the impact of technology on the economy, public safety, and family life.

Communication

1. Comprehend and interpret written, oral, and visual language in a variety of forms for real-life purposes.

    Understand forms of communication specific to the workplace, such as forms, diagrams, manuals, graphs, directions, correspondence, resumes, and presentations. Recognize the purpose and intent of a variety of forms of communication.

2. Express ideas through written, oral, and visual language for a variety of real-life purposes and audiences.

    Apply a process approach to express ideas. Produce a variety of forms of communication appropriate to purposes and audiences.

3. Demonstrate interpersonal skills through effective interaction with others.

    Work closely with others to accomplish tasks. Communicate appropriately in pressure situations. Deal effectively with the public.

4. Develop lifelong communication skills necessary to function productively in diversified work groups.

    Assess and synthesize information. Apply critical and inventive thinking when solving problems. Use current technology systems as tools.

Workplace

1. Manage resources of time, money, materials, and energy.
2. Acquire, organize, analyze, and communicate information.
3. Utilize, maintain, and troubleshoot current technologies.
4. Analyze social, organizational, and technological systems.
5. Employ the interpersonal skills of teamwork, leadership, negotiating, and working with diverse populations and cultures.
6. Apply the critical thinking skills of decision making, problem solving, creative thinking, and reasoning.
7. Display the personal qualities of responsibility, self-esteem, sociability, self-management, and integrity.
8. Recognize social and environmental issues to protect, enhance, and preserve the quality of life.

Career Development

1. Demonstrate the role of self-knowledge in career development.

   Identify values, interests, abilities, skills, work environment factors, life roles, and constraints as they relate to an individual's career life.

2. Demonstrate an awareness of the world of work, career opportunities, and career pathways.

   Engage in career-related experiences (career fairs, shadowing, internships, volunteering, informational interviewing, etc.). Demonstrate knowledge of career rewards and requirements. Recognize trends in future jobs, the economy, and the labor market. Assess and use opportunities for lifelong learning. Conduct research using various resources such as print and video.

3. Apply the critical thinking skills of decision making and goal setting as they relate to career development.

   Identify effective decision-making strategies. Use decision-making strategies to set career life goals.

4. Develop personal and professional employment strategies.

   Demonstrate effective employment strategies (resume writing, interviewing, job search techniques, etc.). Demonstrate the ability to maintain employment.

Resource C:
Tech Prep Checklist

Organizing	Responsibility	Planned	In Progress	Completed
Has a consortium been established?	Leaders of participating institutions			
Has a steering committee been established?	Leaders			
Is there a Coordinator/Director of the consortium?	Steering Committee			
Have the functions of the consortium been identified?	Steering Committee			
Has funding for the consortium been secured?	Steering Committee			
Have conditions for consortium membership been identified?	Steering Committee			
Has a written agreement been developed and signed?	Steering Committee			
Have vision and mission statements been developed?	Steering Committee			
Have program parameters been set?	Steering Committee			
Have career clusters been identified for development?	Steering Committee			
Have work teams been created?				
Curriculum	Steering Committee			
Evaluation	Steering Committee			
Promotion	Steering Committee			
Business & Industry	Steering Committee			

(continued)

Organizing	*Responsibility*	*Planned*	*In Progress*	*Completed*
Has an action team been created?	Action Chair			
Are their goals clear?	Action Chair			
Do they have a plan?	Action Chair			
Are they meeting regularly?	Action Chair			
Have building teams been created?	Building Chair			
Are their goals clear?	Building Chair			
Do they have a plan?	Building Chair			
Are they meeting regularly?	Building Chair			
Have articulation teams been created?	Postsecondary Dean			
Have application/integration teams been created?	Postsecondary Dean			

Curriculum	*Responsibility*	*Planned*	*In Progress*	*Completed*
Have core proficiencies been developed?	Curriculum Work Team			
Have the core proficiencies been validated by business & industry?	Curriculum Work Team			
Have the career clusters been defined?	Steering Committee			
Has a sequence of courses (for the core proficiencies) been created?	Action/Building			
Have applied/integrated teaching strategies been initiated?	Action & Building Teams			
Applied Academics	Action & Building Teams			
Team Teaching	Action & Building Teams			
Curriculum Alignment	Action & Building Teams			
Restructured Schools	Action & Building Teams			

Promotion	*Responsibility*	*Planned*	*In Progress*	*Completed*
Has the promotion work team developed a plan?	Promotion Work Team			
Have introductory promotion materials been produced?	Promotion Work Team			
Are the member schools being supplied with appropriate promotional materials?	Promotion Work Team			
Are local audiences being made aware of Tech Prep?	Action & Building Teams			

Business & Industry Involvement	Responsibility	Planned	In Progress	Completed
Is the business & industry involvement work team actively recruiting business representatives to be involved in Tech Prep?				
Representatives on Steering Committee	Bus/Ind Involvement Work Team			
Representatives on Work Teams	Bus/Ind Involvement Work Team			
Validating proficiencies	Bus/Ind Involvement Work Team			
Are local schools involving business/industry in their efforts?				
Classroom Speakers	Action & Building Teams			
Classroom/Work Exchange	Action & Building Teams			
Shadowing/Mentorship/ Internship	Action & Building Teams			

Inservice	Responsibility	Planned	In Progress	Completed
Have the key players in the consortium been inserviced?	Director/Coordinator			
Have the mentor schools identified local groups to receive inservice?	Action Team			
Have arrangements been made to provide this inservice?	Director/Coordinator			

Bibliography and Sources for More Information

This list represents some of the resources available on Tech Prep and related topics.

Bottoms, Gene, Presson, Alice, & Johnson, Mary. (1992). *Making high schools work through integration of academic and vocational education*. Atlanta: Southern Regional Education Board.

Chew, Catherine. (1993). *Tech prep and counseling: A resource guide*. Madison: Center on Education and Work, University of Wisconsin-Madison.

Crabbe, Anne Borland. (1993). *A collaborative approach to tech prep*. Hamlet, NC: Richmond Community College.

Hull, Dan. (1992). *The tech prep resource series: Getting started in tech prep*. Waco, TX: CORD Communications.

Hull, Dan. (1993). *Opening minds, opening doors: The rebirth of American education*. Waco, TX: CORD Communications.

Illinois State Board of Education. (1991). *Illinois tech prep planning strategies*. Springfield: Author.

Law, Charles. (1994). *Tech prep education: A total quality approach*. Lancaster, PA: Technomic.

Parnell, Dale. (1994). *Logolearning: Searching for meaning in education.* Waco, TX: CORD Communications.

Secretary's Commission on Achieving Necessary Skills. (1991a). *Learning a living: A blueprint for high performance.* Washington, DC: Secretary's Commission on Achieving Necessary Skills, U.S. Department of Labor.

U.S. Department of Labor, Employment and Training Administration. (1992). *School-to-work connections: Formulas for success.* Washington, DC: Author.

Wacker, Gabrielle Banick. (1993). *Tech prep: Effective and promising practices guide.* Madison: Center on Education and Work, University of Wisconsin-Madison.

Wirth, Arthur G. (1992). *Education and work for the year 2000: Choices we face.* San Francisco: Jossey-Bass.

We recommend contacting the following resource centers:

National Network for Curriculum Coordination
Sangamon State University
Springfield, Illinois
(217) 768-6375

National Center for Research in Vocational Education
University of California, Berkeley
Berkeley, California
(800) 762-4093

Office of Vocational and Adult Education
U.S. Department of Education
Washington, D.C.
(202) 205-5440

National Tech Prep Network
Center for Occupational Research and Development
Waco, Texas
(800) 972-2766

The following list represents some of the Tech Prep programs that are in full operation:

Tri-County Technical College, South Carolina
Portland Community College, Portland, Oregon
Community College of Rhode Island, Rhode Island
Mount Hood Community College, Oregon

CORWIN
PRESS

The Corwin Press logo — a raven striding across an open book — represents the happy union of courage and learning. We are a professional-level publisher of books and journals for K–12 educators, and we are committed to creating and providing resources that embody these qualities. Corwin's motto is "Success for All Learners."